D1387822

ANTIGONE RISING

ANTIGONE RISING

The Subversive Power of the Ancient Myths

HELEN MORALES

WILDFIRE

First published in Great Britain in 2020 by Wildfire
An imprint of HEADLINE PUBLISHING GROUP

1

Cataloguing in Publication Data is available from the British Library

Hardback ISBN 978 1 4722 7360 4
Trade paperback ISBN 978 1 4722 7361 1

Offset in 12.69/18.14 pt ElectraLT Std Jouve (UK), Milton Keynes

Printed and bound in Great Britain by Clays Ltd, Elcograf S.p.A.

HEADLINE PUBLISHING GROUP
An Hachette UK Company
Carmelite House
50 Victoria Embankment
London EC4Y 0DZ

www.headline.co.uk
www.hachette.co.uk

For Jennie Ransom
and
for my daughter, Athena Boyle

CONTENTS

PREFACE

Clearly the girl has a fierce spirit. . . . She does not yet know how to submit to bad circumstances.
—the old men of Thebes on Antigone
in Sophocles's *Antigone*

Some people can let things go. I can't.
—GRETA THUNBERG[1]

WHEN I WAS A GIRL I WAS LUCKY ENOUGH TO READ A BOOK called the *Tales of the Greek Heroes*. I was enthralled. No one does power and rebellion and love and loathing quite like the gods and mortals of ancient mythology. I liked knowing that the eyes on the peacock's tail are there because when a beloved giant of Hera, the queen of the gods, had been killed, she plucked out his hundred eyes and placed them, in tribute, on her favorite bird. I still love the way that myths open up new ways of looking at the world.

What makes a myth a myth, rather than just a story, is that it has been told and retold over the centuries and has become meaningful to a culture or community.[2] The Greek and Roman myths have become embedded in, and an influential part of, our culture. They form the foundations and scaffolding of the beliefs that shape our politics and our lives. These can be limiting and destructive but also inspirational and liberating.

The myth of Antigone, as told by the Greek playwright Sophocles, is one of the most well known of the Greek myths and one of the most meaningful for feminism and for revolutionary politics.[3] She has become an icon of resistance. Of pitting personal conviction against state law. Of speaking truth to power.

Antigone insists on burying her brother Polynices, who has been killed while fighting against her city, Thebes, even though her uncle Creon, who is ruler of Thebes, expressly forbids the burial and will impose the death penalty for her defiance. Antigone, just a child of thirteen or fourteen or fifteen, stands up to a powerful adult, even when her sister won't and when the citizens of Thebes are too afraid to do so. Antigone also challenges male authority, in the face of Creon's insistence that women are inferior to men and that men should rule over them. She is vulnerable and terrorized, but she breaks the law anyway.

Antigone was first performed in Athens in (we think) 442 BCE. Today, it is performed all over the world; since 2016, it has been staged, with a new purpose, in Ferguson, Missouri, and in New York City. *Antigone in Ferguson* was conceived by

Bryan Doerries after the killing of eighteen-year-old Michael Brown Jr. by a police officer there in 2014. It presents a rehearsed reading of an adaptation of Sophocles's play, followed by a discussion, with community members, police officers, and activists, about social justice and race.[4]

Why not just write a play about the death of Michael Brown? Why turn to *Antigone* to explore this tragedy? Part of the answer must be that using myth allows us to explore extreme situations without risking the crassness of dramatizing the specific events of a young man's death. This was the reason that the ancient Greeks turned to mythology as the material for their tragedies: when they had staged plays about contemporary events, it had proven too painful for the audience to watch. Greek myths also explore difficult subjects about abuses of power and human weaknesses. Being able to explore questions such as what makes good leadership and how to resist state fascism allows audiences to reflect on those issues in relation to particular, local events, at one remove.

Related to this is what the novelist Ralph Ellison called enlargement: myths enlarge people and literary characters when they overlay them with attributes and accomplishments from the figures in the ancient tales.[5] As scholar Patrice Rankine explains, casting his characters as figures from ancient myth enabled Ellison to construct his characters "from outside of a limited, contemporary framework." This gave them "possibilities [that] transcended the limitations that society placed upon them."[6] Seeing a character or person through a kind of dual vision, as himself and in the role of a figure from myth, gives the reader an enhanced prism through which to understand them.

An initiative run by one of my colleagues, Michael Morgan, is a good illustration of this. The Odyssey Project teaches the myth of the return journey from war of the Greek hero Odysseus to a class of incarcerated youth and undergraduates.[7] The students are asked to explore how episodes from the myth resonate with their own experiences. They find powerful the idea that Odysseus makes terrible mistakes that have devastating consequences for his crew but remains a hero and manages to return home, after many years. Perhaps they can be and do something similar if they see themselves as a kind of Odysseus (or Telemachus or Circe—there are many possibilities). Using myth to enlarge their lives gives the students a different sense of who they are and what they can achieve.

Antigone's myth does not end well for anyone, but we'll save that problem for the end of this book. For now, I want to dwell on the courage and endurance of Antigone's character. She risks everything for a cause that she believes in and refuses to be cowed either by powerful politicians or by what anyone else thinks. The spirit of Antigone lives on in Iesha Evans, who was photographed standing firm in her flimsy summer dress while facing a wall of police officers in riot gear in a Black Lives Matter protest in Baton Rouge. It lives on in Malala Yousafzai, who campaigned for the rights of girls in Pakistan to be educated, even though it was dangerous to break the law of the Taliban (who tried, unsuccessfully, to kill her in 2012). And it lives on in the resolute opposition to climate change shown by Greta Thunberg, who, at sixteen years old, went on strike from school to protest outside the Swedish parliament: once a lone figure with a cardboard sign, now the inspiration for a global movement.

The "girl against the world" scenario has a glamorous appeal; we like it when the underdog triumphs. Sophocles's *Antigone* is frequently taught in high schools in the United States, and whenever I speak about the play in local schools, the students are clearly on the side of Antigone. She is a heroine, they say, and Creon is a total fascist who deserves everything he gets.

It is unlikely that the play's original audience would have been so one-sided in their sympathies. The Greeks would likely have been more critical of Antigone, a girl who spoke and acted out of turn, even as many would have also recognized the failings of the king, Creon.

A medical text from the time called *On the Diseases of Virgins* tells us that girls in Antigone's situation, who were old enough to be married but had not yet taken husbands, were thought to be diseased.[8] They went mad and had visions of death. In *Antigone*, Antigone longs for death; she obsessively imagines her own death and tells us that she welcomes it. Much is also made of the fact that she is unmarried, despite being old enough to be married. Her name is a clue: it can mean against (*anti*) procreation (*gonē*). The medical text gives us a new frame through which to understand Antigone's resolve. Instead of seeing her as a heroine who is determined to do the right thing, even if she risks being put to death, we now see her as showing symptoms of the "disease of young girls," as dysfunctional, unhinged, mad.

Sometimes simply juxtaposing ancient and modern can reveal new and unexpected perspectives. Greta Thunberg's behavior has also been pathologized: she has been criticized and belittled for having Asperger's syndrome. It has made her, critics say, more open to exploitation by others. But Thunberg herself has spoken about how having Asperger's has helped with her activism: it is a gift that "makes her see things outside the box."[9] She has not allowed herself to be defined negatively but has turned the pathology around into something positive. Perhaps we can also take this approach with Antigone. We can understand her madness and dysfunction, as some ancients would have seen it, as giving Antigone a political edge, as enabling her not to fear death, and as fueling her single-mindedness. Through this lens, ancient myths don't just enlarge human stories; modern figures and events can also invite us to see the ancient myths in new ways.

For the ancient Greeks and Romans, the gods were more than just exciting characters. Most worshipped them and took religious rituals very seriously.[10] But, there is a crucial difference between ancient Greek and Roman religious practice and the main religions practiced today. Unlike our monotheistic religions of Christianity, Islam, and Judaism, Greek and Roman religion was polytheistic. Zeus or Jupiter (as the Greeks and Romans called him, respectively) was the most powerful god, and it was sensible not to get on the wrong side of his thunderbolt, but all of the gods demanded worship, and there was no religious text or commandments to follow. (When Antigone appeals to the eternal and unwritten laws, what she means is unclear, which is part of the problem).

A couple of key things follow from this. The first is that mythological narratives became a way of thinking through complicated moral dilemmas. This makes them useful for us too; we keep returning to Greek and Roman myths precisely because they avoid the simple "good versus evil" stories, from fairy tales to Disney movies, that are such a strong part of our culture. Second, myths, especially those that were told in epic poetry and drama, were widely known and authoritative. All educated, and many uneducated, Greek and Romans would have known their Homer. We don't have anything like this: when I asked my class of seven hundred students, the book that was familiar to most of them was not the Bible or the Koran or Shakespeare or Walt Whitman—but Dr. Seuss.

The cultural authority of epic and tragedy continued through the advent of Christianity as a major religion. Christian texts often rewrote Greek and Roman myths to give them a different message. Greek and Roman mythology, and classical antiquity more broadly, have been enormously influential in Western culture and beyond.[11] By classical antiquity I mean the period when Greek and Roman cultures flourished in the lands that we now call Europe, North Africa, and Western Asia, from the eighth century BCE, when the epic poems of Homer were first sung, to the fifth century CE, when what we now call the Middle Ages began. (I'm all too aware of the fast leaps across time and space and how imprecise a phrase *Greek and Roman* can be.) Intellectual history, by which I mean the major philosophers, novelists, theorists, playwrights, politicians, and other thinkers from antiquity to today, has continually drawn on Greek and Roman myths. That means that for us to enter into conversations—philosophical, historical, artistic, and political—more often than not involves engaging with ideas and arguments from ancient Greece and Rome.

The ideological purpose of these conversations has varied widely. Classical antiquity has been used to justify fascism, slavery, white supremacy, and misogyny. It has also played a crucial role in political idealism, inspiring, variously, the Founding Fathers (and influencing foundational statements such as the Declaration of Independence and the US Constitution), trades union movements, Marxism, and the gay rights movement.[12] As ancient historian Neville Morley writes of classical antiquity, in his book *Classics: Why It Matters*, "There is always a struggle over its ownership, and who gets to claim and define it."[13] So maybe we're due for a fresh understanding of how ancient Greek and Roman myths, and their characters, can be claimed and defined by all of us who want to resist the current movement toward greater patriarchal control and who are working to make this a more equal, empathetic, and enlightened world.

This book brings together two parts of my life: my professional self and my role as a mother. I have been researching and teaching ancient mythology for over twenty-five years, in universities in England and the United States. It is through teaching the myths to my students that I have seen how powerful these tales are and how reading them critically and creatively can be empowering. Telling new stories is, of course, essential, but viewing our worlds through the lens of the old myths is also meaningful.

I am also the mother of a teenage daughter, Athena. She and her friends have been taught about ancient Greece and its myths and culture but without any understanding that what they were learning had much relevance to their lives today, be-yond vague notions of inheriting democracy. This book grew from my attempts to explain to Athena that the things that were preoccupying her and her peer group—girls' safety, school dress codes, and dieting, as well as dealing with a changing political climate in which their freedoms were being curtailed and environmental protections reversed—are all underpinned by cultural narratives. One of the planks in this ideological scaffolding is classical mythology. Part of being empowered and fighting back involves understanding these myths and their cultural impact and turning them to our own advantage.

In each of the chapters, the relationship between ancient and modern is different. In some, specific Greek and Roman texts take center stage: Aristophanes's *Lysistrata*, Sophocles's *Antigone*, and Ovid's *Metamorphoses*. We will look at how they have been read, and misread, to serve (or resist) progres-sive agendas. The chapter on dieting will argue that the an-cient Greek doctor Hippocrates has been misunderstood and misquoted in modern medical and popular writing on diets: the relationship between ancient and modern here is specific and clear, as the ancient is appropriated by the modern in ways that are especially hurtful to women. This chapter and the one on controlling women also give us some insight into ancient attitudes toward women, beyond what can be gleaned from myth.

In the first chapter, and the chapter on school dress codes and the policing of women's dress by the "women controllers" of ancient Greece, the relationship between ancient and modern is looser; it is one of congruence rather than direct influence. Or, to put it another way, direct influence across swathes of time and space is difficult to map. Sometimes it is impossible to trace the precise origins of an idea or behavior to ancient Greece or Rome, but more often than not we have no idea whether something originated there or whether it was passed down to them from another culture or whether indeed it had many different origins.[14] Tracing precise historical genealogies is not the point of the book. Recognizing entrenched cultural patterns is.

In the second half of the book, I turn to consider the very different and striking ways in which the superstar Beyoncé, novelist Ali Smith, and Mexican vigilante killer Diana, the Hunter of Bus Drivers, have reimagined ancient myths as acts of resistance: resistance toward tired and damaging misogynist myths, including racist and transphobic ones.

These re-creations of ancient myths ask over and over: Who owns classical antiquity? Who owns culture? The response: We do.

ONE

KILLING AMAZONS

THIS BOOK STARTS WHERE MISOGYNY ENDS, WITH MEN KILL-
ing women. We will come to the reality of men killing women
(and men) shortly, but I want to begin with the fantasy. I want
to begin with one of the earliest fantasies of killing women
ever recorded: ancient Greek myths about killing Amazons.

The Amazons were warrior women from faraway lands
and some of the most fearsome adversaries of the heroes of
Greek myth.[1] They were reputed to be "the equals of men."[2]
According to one mythological tale, the hero Hercules was
sent on a quest to recover the girdle of the Amazon queen
Hippolyta. (*Girdle* makes it sound like an ancient version of
Spanx; war-belt is probably a better description.) He stabs or
bludgeons her to death and steals the belt. Some versions of
the story describe how Hercules kills Amazon, after Amazon,

We don't need another hero. (Achilles kills Penthesilea, amphora by the Exekias painter from around 530 BCE.)

after Amazon: Aella, Philippis, Prothoe, Eriboea, Celaeno, Eurybia, Phoebe, Deianeira, Asteria, Tecmessa, Alcippe, and Melanippe.[3]

The Greek hero Achilles killed the Amazon Penthesilea when the Amazons joined forces with the Trojans to fight the Greeks in the Trojan War. In one version of the story, she is on horseback, and he spears her with such force that the weapon goes through the woman and her horse together. Others tell how he fell in love with her as she was dying and even that he desired and desecrated her corpse.[4]

The Greek hero Bellerophon killed many Amazons by flying above them on his winged horse and dropping boulders on them until they were crushed to death.

Killing Amazons

The Greek hero . . . well, you get the picture. Killing Amazons was part of what made Greek heroes, heroes. As Mary Beard puts it: "The basic message was that the only good Amazon was a dead one."[5] This message was pressed home repeatedly in ancient Greece. Images of dead or dying Amazons were displayed inside people's homes (in the vase paintings that survive, Amazons are the second-most-popular subject; Hercules is the first) and on public monuments such as the Parthenon temple in Athens.

There is a relationship between the ancient fantasy of killing women and the modern reality. On the evening of Friday, May 23, 2014, I was at home, grading papers. I had been a professor in the Classics Department at the University of California, Santa Barbara for five years, and although I enjoyed the job in general, I hated grading papers. To relieve the boredom, I skimmed articles in an online newspaper. I was looking for celebrity gossip but found instead the breaking news that there had been a massacre in Isla Vista, an area next to the campus where many students live. I phoned colleagues and emailed graduate students. We scrambled for information: Was everyone safe?

We would gradually learn that six students—George Chen, Cheng Yuan "James" Hong, Weihan "David" Wang, Katherine Breann Cooper, Christopher Ross Michaels-Martinez, and Veronika Elizabeth Weiss—were murdered in what would become known as the Isla Vista killings. Fourteen other students were injured before the killer shot himself. Katie Cooper and Christopher Michaels-Martinez took classes in our department; Katie was interested in art history and archaeology, and Christopher in English literature and Classics. One of my colleagues had just met with Christopher to discuss the prospect of him spending a year abroad in Rome. Another was teaching an ancient Greek class that had started out with seven students in it, including Katie, and that now had six. In every ancient Greek class that we have taught since, I see the absence of Katie Cooper, golden girl, frozen forever at the age of twenty-two.

I remember the next days and weeks as a series of dazed snapshots: the bravery of Richard Martinez, Christopher's father, as he urged the mourning crowd to chant "not one more"; a colleague at a department memorial talking about Katie Cooper's sense of joy and fun and how he would be proud if his daughter grew up to be like Katie; the dean suggesting that we teach students to find solace in art and literature, although the friends of the students who had died could barely function. My daughter, Athena, was then thirteen years old. Five years earlier we had moved to California from England, where hooliganism, public drunkenness, and stabbings are serious problems but not gun violence. She had many questions: Was she safe at school? Was I likely to get shot? Why would someone do this?

I first knew I would write this book when a young man whose name should not be given the oxygen of publicity killed our students. Did the availability of guns and the perpetrator's mental health problems contribute to the killings? Yes and yes. Undoubtedly. But the killer's views about women, fomented by seething resentments in online "pickup artist" sites and detailed in a one-hundred-and-forty-page manifesto that he emailed to people before the massacre, were what drove him to kill.

These views go back to antiquity, and some of the beliefs about women that we have inherited from ancient Greece and Rome form the imaginative scaffolding that underpins our beliefs about women today. To ignore that history blinds us to how entrenched some violent social structures really are. The first step toward understanding, and therefore doing something to prevent, misogyny is to recognize how and where it is culturally hardwired. The killings in Isla Vista were the work of one individual, "a quiet, troubled loner."[6] But they were also the work of thousands of years of our telling the same stories about the relationships between men and women, desire, and control.

In her book *Down Girl*, philosopher Kate Manne explains what misogyny is and how it works.[7] It is best understood, she writes, "as primarily a property of social environments in which women are liable to encounter hostility due to the enforcement and policing of patriarchal norms and expectations—often, though not exclusively, insofar as they violate patriarchal law and order. Misogyny hence functions to enforce and police women's subordination and to uphold male dominance, against the backdrop of other intersecting systems of oppression and vulnerability, dominance and disadvantage."[8]

Her analysis moves us away from thinking of misogyny as *an attitude* toward women that individual men and women may hold, toward thinking of it as *social forces* that police norms and expectations of a patriarchal world. Misogyny is the "'law enforcement' branch of a patriarchal order, which has the overall function of *policing* and *enforcing* its governing ideology."[9] One of the main ways in which misogyny does this is by differentiating between "good women" and "bad women" and punishing the "bad women."

In ancient Greek myth, Amazons were considered to be bad women. They were bad because they rejected marriage. Marriage was expected of all good Greek women. Good women married, had children, and tended house, roles that kept them subservient to men. Amazons, in contrast, lived as nomads, traveling from place to place. They fought battles. They enjoyed sexual relations with men when and how they wanted them (one story tells how it took Alexander the Great thirteen days to satisfy the desire of the Amazon Thalestris), but they did not live with men. They were manless, or man-free, and they were punished for it.[10]

The Isla Vista killer also punished women for not wanting to be with him: "I don't know why you girls aren't attracted to me," he whined in his manifesto, "but I will punish you all for it. . . . Who's the alpha male now, bitches?" He wrote about the need to control women's sexual behavior: "Women should not have the choice of who to mate with. That choice should be made for them by civilized men of intelligence."[11] The outspoken clinical psychologist Jordan Peterson has argued that the "rational solution" to prevent men like the Isla Vista killer from committing violent acts is "enforced monogamy."[12] He does not see that enforced monogamy is itself a violent act.

It is through the punishment of sexually renegade women that Greek heroes earned their superstar status. Hercules's quest for the war-belt of the Amazon Hippolyta was one of his twelve labors, tasks that were set as a punishment for domestic violence: "in a fit of madness," he had killed his wife, Megara, and their children.[13] Upon successful completion of the labors, Hercules would be cleansed of his crime (note the sour logic: to expiate for killing a woman, he killed more women). On his death, his father, Zeus, king of the gods, raised him up to Mount Olympus: in death, as in life, Hercules was a demigod.

Part of the Isla Vista killer's delusion was that through punishing the women whose love he felt entitled to, he would become heroic, semidivine. Violence against women is integral to heroism, or at least a particular kind of macho heroism. The Isla Vista killer wanted to be a Hercules, "more than human . . . the closest thing there is to a living god" an "alpha male," as he put it in his online manifesto. He wanted women to adore him; he also wanted to be superior to other men. His method of achieving this may have been exceptional, but the desire itself is not.[14] Of course, we say that the killer had mental health problems. That's what ancient writers said about Hercules, too, when he killed his wife and children. Perhaps it is hard to tell the difference between delusion and disorder and hyperheroism.

An essential part of the myth of the Amazons was that the warrior women were foreign, not Greek. The fantasy was not just of men getting the better of women but of *Greek* men getting the better of *foreign* women. Killing Amazons was a performance of ethnic as well as sexual superiority. For the Isla Vista killer, destroying women was driven by an ideology of white supremacy. He set out to kill what he desired, "a beautiful blonde girlfriend." He himself was born from a Malaysian Chinese mother and a white British father, and his manifesto railed against black and brown men who do not deserve, in his view, the attentions of blonde white women. These wars on women, ancient and modern, were propelled by racial as well as sexual hatred. They are far from unusual in this respect.[15]

Part of what was so beguiling about the Amazons was that they led lives of sexual equality. Unlike the real women who lived in ancient Greece, Amazons enjoyed the same freedoms that men did. They enjoyed relationships with men, but they did not need them, sexually or politically. "Who could believe that an army of women, or a city, or a tribe, could ever be organized without men?" exclaimed one Greek writer.[16]

This is why, in the nineteenth century, first-wave feminists like Elizabeth Cady Stanton looked to the Amazons as a model for matriarchy: rule by women.[17] One of these feminists was a woman called Sadie Elizabeth Holloway. Educated at Mount

Holyoke, a women's college, Holloway went on to become an attorney and psychologist. Together with her husband, William Moulton Marston, she did some extraordinary things, including developing an early version of the lie detector test. In 1941, inspired by Holloway and Olive Byrne, the woman with whom they both had love affairs, Marston created a modern superhero Amazon: Wonder Woman.

Wonder Woman, aka Princess Diana of Themyscira, daughter of Hippolyta, is an Amazon who is finally allowed to live, helped by her extraordinary strength, "integrity and humanity,"[18] and a golden lasso that can tell when men are lying (Holloway and Marston's lie detector test immortalized as their superhero's weapon). Played on-screen by former Miss World America, Lynda Carter, and former Miss Israel, Gal Gadot, Wonder Woman became, for a few months in 2014, the United Nations' honorary ambassador for the empowerment of women and girls. She was removed after protestors pointed out that the comic book character's whiteness, pinup girl looks, and American flag costume made her an inappropriate choice for the role.

One of the United Nations' goals was gender equality for all women and girls by 2030 and essential to achieving that goal is education. But getting an education can be a dangerous business for women. The Isla Vista killer ended up murdering women and men, but his chief target was a sorority house. He did not just want to kill women; he wanted to kill women students. In this, he was the copycat of another killer, who in 1989 murdered fourteen women in the so-called Montreal massacre at the École Polytechnique, an engineering school affiliated with the University of Montreal. The Montreal killer entered the building, separated the men from the women, and shot the women with a semiautomatic rifle, announcing that he was "fighting feminism." He, who, like the Isla Vista killer, had dropped out of college, thought that women should not study engineering. He was enraged by feminists whom he saw as taking advantages that men had (like education) while also hanging on to those that they had (like, he said, extended maternity leave). Therefore, he explained, "I have decided to send the feminists, who have always ruined my life, to their Maker . . . I have decided to put an end to those viragos."[19] An interesting choice of word: *virago* originally meant "warrior woman" or "Amazon" before it changed over time to mean "domineering woman" or "shrew"—the linguistics of misogyny.

Elsewhere, girls who try to get an education are targeted en masse. In Afghanistan and Pakistan, the Taliban outlawed education for girls over the age of eight, and that education consisted only of learning the Koran. They shot the activist Malala Yousafzai in retaliation for her and her family's work promoting girls' education. The Nigeria-based terrorist group Boko Haram has prevented many girls from finishing their education. In 2014, its members kidnapped 276 girls from their high school in the town of Chibok. In 2018, they kidnapped 110 schoolgirls from the Government Girls' Science and Technical College in Dapchi, in northeast Nigeria. Many of the girls were forced into marriages. According to UNICEF, Boko Haram has destroyed more than fourteen hundred schools and killed 2,295 teachers. The name Boko Haram means "education is forbidden."[20] Without education, without being able to study at a school or university free of harassment from entitled men and free of violence by entitled men, gender equality is impossible.

The Isla Vista killings sparked a social media campaign: #YesAllWomen. The thinking behind it was that even if not all men are violent misogynists like the Isla Vista killer (as some men rushed to say, as if it was all about them), all women are affected by violent misogyny, in the workplace, walking down the street, and in their intimate relationships. On Twitter, women told the truth about their everyday fears of male violence.

You could be forgiven for thinking that, living as we do in the enlightened era of #YesAllWomen and #MeToo and during a time of brilliant and incisive analysis on gender and violence by Rebecca Solnit and Chimamanda Ngozi Adichie and by Sara Ahmed and Kate Manne, we would have a heightened awareness about how misogyny leads to women being killed. You would think that we would be primed to avoid the next school massacre. You would think.

This is Athena's #YesAllWomen story.

When Athena was in middle school, she visited the local public high school, about one and a half miles from Isla Vista, as a prospective student. She shadowed a tenth grader, an energetic and outgoing girl whom we'll call Laura. The day began uneventfully; Athena enjoyed a class on *To Kill a Mockingbird* and took a chemistry test. At recess, however, while she and

Laura were talking, an older boy came up to Laura, ground his crotch against her, and said something crude about her chest. Laura kicked him in the shin and told him to fuck off. "Don't worry," she said to Athena. "It happens every day."

Athena did not attend that high school. (I am well aware of what a privilege it is to have a choice about her schooling.) If she had, she might have been involved in the following incident in January 2018. Six boys from the school made a video and posted it in an online chat room. It is a ninety-second mock instructional video in which one of the students says, "I'm going to show you how to kill a thot." (Thot, pronounced "thought," is an acronym for "that ho over there." It is a slur used against a woman for being promiscuous and is often used to insult lower-class and black women.[21]) The boy then points a rifle at the camera and explains how to use it. He then demonstrates how to inflict greater harm by attaching and using a bayonet. The video ends with him saying: "I hope you found this video useful in your war against thots." The video was posted to a private chat room, where another of the six boys posted a kill list of "thots that need to be eradicated," alongside the names of at least sixteen girls from all three public high schools in Santa Barbara and that of a twelve-year-old from a local middle school.

Details of what happened next remain elusive because the privacy of boys who are minors is protected even when the safety of girls who are minors is not. From what we can glean from parents of the children, one parent saw the video and reported the boys to the school authorities. The boy who published the kill list has since been convicted of making a terrorist threat, his original felony charge having been reduced to a misdemeanor. The boy who described how to gut girls with a bayonet has, according to several parents, never been charged with a crime.[22] Another one of the six boys in the chat room, whose post allegedly contained swastika flags and Nazi tanks, has, according to parents, not been charged.[23] One mother of a girl on the kill list has moved her daughter to a different school. The local newspaper reports that "she said the chat-room incident traumatized her daughter. She's come home after school in tears. Her hair started falling out. She lost a lot of sleep. And in each of her classes, she'd plan where she could run or hide."[24]

Men and boys killing and fantasizing about killing women and girls as punishments for not needing men, for not being under men's sexual control, for daring to be educated, for living freely. Men and boys, long ago and only last year, killing women and girls (and men who get in their way) in their imaginations, in chat rooms, and in the streets. And yet still we fail to recognize the fantasies as dangerous. The police investigated the six boys who called girls thots and drew up a kill list. They determined that the boys posed "no immediate threat." According to parents, by the end of that week the boys were back in the classroom.

It is not necessary, when trying to understand violent acts like the Isla Vista killings, to look to antiquity and to see them in relation to the Greek myths about killing Amazons. I have worried about whether it is a crass move to make: too academic, too contrived. I have decided to risk that criticism because turning to the ancient material helps us, I think, to see how long-standing and, therefore, how hard to banish certain cultural narratives are. My hope is that discerning this bigger picture will make us less likely to dismiss the killings of women as isolated incidents and the work of a few crazed men. My hope is that by tracing patterns and connections between ancient and modern beliefs and practices it will become easier to understand how misogyny operates and the ways in which classical antiquity plays a role (although it is not the only player and this is not its only role) in legitimating how misogyny operates today. It is a small hope. Ancient Amazons can be resurrected as Wonder Woman, but I am well aware that nothing will bring back the six students killed near their university in 2014.

TWO

NO PEACE, NO PIECE!

AFTER YEARS OF INTERNAL WARFARE IN GREECE, THE STORY
goes, Lysistrata persuades the women of opposing city-states to
band together and go on a sex strike. Until the men put aside
their weapons, their wives will deny them sex (including doing it in the "lioness on the cheese grater position"—what exactly this refers to remains one of antiquity's great mysteries).
Scenes of comic slapstick laced with political insight follow.
In the end, the men can take it no longer and agree to stop
fighting. The women of Greece and their sex strike have won.
The "no peace, no piece!" strategy has worked.

The playwright Aristophanes first told this story in his comedy *Lysistrata*, written twenty years into the Greek conflict
known as the Peloponnesian War, in the fifth century BCE.[1]
His comedies, like all Athenian dramas, were performed to
the men of Athens in big civic festivals with much fanfare and

religious ritual. They regularly grappled with contemporary issues and pilloried politicians, like *Saturday Night Live*, but more outrageous (Aristophanes claims to have been fined for his personal attacks on politicians) and more sexually explicit.[2]

From far-fetched fantasy to political blueprint, *Lysistrata* has become an iconic myth of feminist protest. It has been taken up in film and art, from the Swedish film *The Girls* (1968), in which women who are performing *Lysistrata* in a traveling theater group are inspired to make changes in their own lives,[3] to Tony Harrison's play *A Common Chorus* (1992), set in the women's peace camp at Greenham Common nuclear missile base,[4] to Germaine Greer's play *Lysistrata—The Sex Strike* (first performed in 1999), in which the actions of the ancient Greek women are used to critique the lack of intersectionality in women's activism today as well as push for peace.[5] In 2003, the Lysistrata Project, founded by two feminist pacifists from New York, protested against the Iraq War with more than one thousand readings of *Lysistrata* performed across the globe on a single day.[6]

The idea that a sex strike is an effective means of protest—and not just a trope to be explored through art—has gained some traction. In May 2019, actor and activist Alyssa Milano called for women in the United States to go on sex strike in protest of the strict new antiabortion laws passed by the legislatures of six states, Georgia, Kentucky, Ohio, Mississippi, Iowa, and North Dakota, that prohibit abortion after six weeks or when cardiac activity is first detected. She tweeted:

No Peace, No Piece!

Our reproductive rights are being erased.

Until women have legal control over our own bodies we just cannot risk pregnancy.

JOIN ME by not having sex until we get bodily autonomy back.

I'm calling for a #SexStrike.

To bolster her proposal, Milano shared on Twitter an online article from Quartz news organization called "History Shows That Sex Strikes Are a Surprisingly Effective Strategy for Political Change."[7] The piece highlighted several sex strikes, including one in the African country of Liberia in 2003. Milano followed this by cowriting an op-ed in which she reiterated that "Lysistratic protest is a long standing, effective and empowering method to fight for change."[8] Beyond op-eds debating the value of sex strikes, nothing came of Milano's call to sex strike.

A few years before Milano's tweet, the movie director Spike Lee had urged female students to stage a sex strike to stop men sexually harassing and raping women on university and college campuses in the United States. This happened in 2015, during a publicity tour for his movie adaptation of the Lysistrata myth, *Chi-Raq*.[9] The film, so named because the death toll in Chicago rivals that in war-torn Iraq, is an extravagant, explosive, musical version, set in Chicago's South Side. Ancient Greek verse can be quite like modern rap, as Samuel L. Jackson's flamboyant one-man Greek chorus shows:

ANTIGONE RISING

In the year 411 BC — that's before baby Jesus
* y'all — the great Aristophanes penned a play*
satirizing his day
and in the style of his time
'stophanes made that shit rhyme.
That's why today we retain his verse
To show our love for the universe.
But warning — you gonna see some PAIN.

The pain is caused by the gang warfare between the Spartans, led by rapper Demetrius Dupree aka Chi-Raq (played by Nick Cannon), and the Trojans led by the Cyclops (Wesley Snipes). A young girl, Patti, is killed; the scenes of mourning are given a special poignancy by the casting of Jennifer Hudson, whose own mother and brother were murdered with guns, as Patti's mother. Chi-Raq's girlfriend, Lysistrata (Teyonnah Parris), is urged by a neighbor, Miss Helen (Angela Bassett), to look up "sex strike" on the web. She finds a film about the sex strike in Liberia, and it inspires her to rally the women of Chicago into staging their own sex strike. They are successful, although the script diverges from the ancient myth in a significant way.

But what exactly is a sex strike? (Marriage is not a satisfactory answer.) In the ancient Greek myth, Lysistrata describes it in the following way:

If we sat around at home all made-up, and walked past the men wearing only our diaphanous underwear, with our pubes plucked in a neat triangle, and our husbands got

Spike Lee urges women students to sex strike. (Discussing his film *Chi-Raq* in 2015.)

hard and hankered to ball us, but we didn't go near them and kept away, they'd sue for peace, and pretty quick, you can count on that![10]

This is more of a climax strike than a sex strike, which is to say that many of the components of sex—such as titillation and physical closeness—are there, just not the actual consummation. It is less a withdrawal from sex than a prolonged tease. We would not call strip clubs sex-strike clubs.

The sex strike in Liberia that inspired both Alyssa Milano and Spike Lee's heroine was a very different kind of protest and not at all characterized by women gyrating and teasing men. One of its leaders was Leymah Gbowee, who was awarded the Nobel Peace Prize in 2011 for her campaigning for peace. The Western media labeled her the "Liberian Lysistrata." Journalists have focused on her organization of a sex strike, with comments such as: "Employing the strength of Lysistrata, and Aristophanes' heroines of the Peloponnesian War, they withheld sex from their men" (Huffington Post), and "self-assured and instinctively political, Gbowee is a modern-day Lysistrata" (Gossip Central). A report in the British newspaper the *Daily Telegraph* went even further and suggested a *causal* relationship between the character Lysistrata's activism in ancient Greece (which they mistake for being a historical event rather than fiction) and Leymah Gbowee's activism in Liberia: "She persuaded many Liberian women to withhold sex from their warring menfolk unless they came to the negotiating table, a devastatingly successful campaign inspired by Aristophanes' Lysistrata, who used the same strategy during the Peloponnesian War."[11]

In fact, the sex strike was a very small part of the Liberian women's activism. In her memoir *Mighty Be Our Powers*, Leymah Gbowee devotes less than a page to it:

> "Sex Strike" is the headline that sells, so when reporters interview me, they tend to ask about the sex strike first. Did the women of Liberia really bring an end to the heinous

civil war by withholding sex? Well, it certainly gave the men a fresh motive to press for peace. But the truth is that the greatest weapons of the Liberian women's movement were moral clarity, persistence, and patience. Nothing happened overnight. In fact it took three years of community awareness, sit-ins, and nonviolent demonstrations staged by ordinary "market women"—years of gathering in the roads in eye-catching white T-shirts, demanding the attention of convoys of officials and media folks who would glimpse the signs and the dancing, would hear the chanting and the singing. Then we launched the sex strike. In 2002, Liberia's Christian and Muslim women banded together to refuse sex with their husbands until the violence and the civil strife ended.[12]

The sex strike was a minor element in a more prolonged and complex campaign of protest. In Gbowee's account, a pivotal moment in that campaign came in June 2003, after she had led a delegation of women to Accra in Ghana where the warring factions were holding peace talks. The talks dragged on for weeks, until the women formed a human barricade outside the meeting room and refused to let the men out until they had agreed on peace. Gbowee, accused of obstructing justice and facing arrest, threatened to strip naked. In West African society, a woman taking off her clothes as a gesture of protest performs a curse upon the men who see her: "For this group of men to see a woman naked would be almost like a death sentence."[13] Her intervention was successful: the men went back into the room and negotiated an end to the war.[14] Referring to Leymah Gbowee as the Liberian Lysistrata and reducing the women's resistance to a sex strike are crass distortions that obscure the work that really went into securing peace.

Sex strike is a largely bogus category: it is a term that seems straightforward, but when you examine it, it means different things in different contexts. As in the Liberian sex strike, sex strikes in Colombia in 2011 (to compel the government to repair a road) and in Kenya in 2009 (to end government in-fighting) were successful primarily because they attracted publicity and so *shamed* or otherwise put pressure on those in power to take action, not because women withholding sex *frustrated* men into changing their behavior. The emphasis for the Colombian women was not on the withdrawal of sex for pleasure but on their refusal to get pregnant until they could safely travel to a hospital to give birth: "We are being deprived of our most basic human rights and we cannot allow that to happen. Why bring children into this world when they can just die without medical attention and we can't even offer them the most basic rights? We just decided to stop having sex and stop having children until the state fulfills its previous promises."[15] Despite all this, the Western media framed these women as modern-day Lysistratas.[16]

The term *sex strike* nearly always applies to women; men never seem to go on sex strike. It implies, then, that sex is a kind of work, performed by women for men, that women only have sex to please men, and that for a woman to withhold sex is a similar kind of political action to labor stoppages by unionized workers. Also, as classicist Donna Zuckerberg comments, "a sex strike rests on the premise that women are not full political actors and still need to exercise their influence through the domestic sphere."[17] This is all a pretty outdated view of heterosexual relationships.

It also raises an obvious question: If a so-called sex strike is, in part at least, about denying men (in the words of *Chi-Raq*'s Lysistrata) "rights of access and entrance," then would we not expect some men to seek that in some other way, by going to prostitutes, for example, or taking male lovers, or by raping their wives and girlfriends? (In the Greek myth, Lysistrata prepares the women for the likelihood that they might be forced, in which case, she advises, they should "submit grudgingly and not thrust back.")

I put this question to Leymah Gbowee, while she was visiting the university where I work, a few days before it was announced that she had won the Nobel Prize. She was forthcoming about the practicalities of the sex strike. She explained that when the strike was first suggested, by a Muslim woman, it was not taken seriously. "We all thought she was mad," she told me. "We wondered whether she could truly be a Muslim!" After discussion, it won favor as a means of making every man participate in the protest: "The message was that while the fighting continued, no one was innocent—not doing anything to stop it made you guilty,"[18] It worked best, said Gbowee, in rural communities where the women put a strong religious spin on their actions, but in urban communities, once the strike had started, women came to meetings with bruises on their faces. They had certainly been assaulted and likely also raped.

This is the reality of sex strikes. It is one reason why Spike Lee's call for female students to go on sex strike to prevent men from raping them on university campuses is so irresponsible. The ancient myth, as conveyed in newspapers' comparisons and headlines, is an unhelpful frame; it imposes Aristophanes's comedic fantasy template onto episodes of modern political activism. Once cast in these terms, it is hard for modern protests to break free from the template; it takes on the cultural authority with which we invest classical myth. The go-to trope of click-bait articles becomes a distorting mirror that reduces women to bodies and complex political action to titillation.

At the end of our interview I asked Gbowee whether she had ever read *Lysistrata*. She said that she had but only recently. She had won an award, and a friend gave her a copy of the play as a celebratory gift. I asked her what she thought about the play and the comparisons that have been made in the press. She said nothing but gave me a long look of unmitigated contempt.

So how is the myth of Lysistrata useful to us? There are progressive political insights in Aristophanes's play, but the problem is that these are spliced between jokes about erections and repeated threats by the men, played for laughs, to slap, punch, and set fire to the women. These shifts of subject

matter, tenor, and tone make it hard for the audience to respond from a steady perspective. If we mine the play for its politics, we're missing the joke; if we just laugh at the dick jokes,
we're missing the point.

The ending of *Lysistrata* provides the most striking example of these rapid shifts. Our heroine oversees the negotia-
tions between the delegates from the warring cities, and she
brings in a naked woman called Reconciliation, who is both
an allegory and an exotic dancer. (On the Athenian stage,
it is likely that a male dancer dressed up as a naked woman
would have played the role.) Lysistrata imparts wisdom to
each of the delegates, trying to get them to see the situation
from the other's perspective. But it is the nude body of Reconciliation that persuades the men, not Lysistrata's rhetoric.
Their attention is riveted to the naked woman, whose body
they divide up, as they divide up the Greek territory, with
"I'll give you the two hills if I can have the valley" kind of
humor. For modern readers and viewers, this scene invokes
today's post-truth politics—it doesn't matter what is *said*, it's
the emotional appeal of the visual that counts. The ending
poses valuable questions about protest and what makes a protest successful. Is it enough to get the desired outcome by any
means possible, or is it also important to win the *arguments*?

The ending undermines Lysistrata's authority (even though
it was her ploy to bring Reconciliation), and most modern
productions and adaptations cut or alter these final scenes.
Chi-Raq makes a radical change to the story by ending not
with a sexy dance and division of the gangland territory but

with the promise of jobs and medical care for everyone, a gun amnesty, and truth and reconciliation for the victims. Chi-Raq learns about his family legacy of murder and hands himself in to the police for the killing he committed. The story and the tone change as we move from the comedy of *Lysistrata* to the tragedy of *Oedipus Rex*, in which the king exiles himself for crimes he committed and thereby saves his city.[19]

But the ending of the play is arguably not the most important scene. In the middle of the drama, Lysistrata gives a speech on how she thinks that politics ought to be handled. Using a domestic metaphor, she says, "If you had any sense, you would handle all your affairs in the way we handle wool," and explains:

> First of all, just like washing out a raw fleece, you should wash the sheep-dung out of the body politic in a bath, then put it on a bed, beat out the villains with a stick and pick off the burrs; and as for those people who combine and mat themselves together to gain office, you should card them out and pluck off the heads. Then card the wool into the work-basket of union and concord, mixing in everyone; and the immigrants, and any foreigner who's friendly to you, and anyone who's in debt to the treasury, they should be mixed in as well . . . and then make a great ball of wool, and from that weave a warm cloak for the people to wear.[20]

This is a clarion call for an inclusive politics, one that binds together citizens, immigrants, and foreigners (including those who are in debt) and excludes self-serving politicians and other villains. In today's climate, it sounds like the manifesto of a political visionary.

Also visionary is the activism of the older women in the play. The older women take over the Acropolis, where the wealth of Athens was stored. They take control of the treasury, explains Lysistrata, "so we could keep the money safe and thereby prevent you from making war."[21] Even the actions of the younger women have an economic dimension. They do not just withdraw sex from their husbands, they also withdraw their unpaid domestic labor; they stop feeding and tending to their children and looking after their homes.

The economic activism of Lysistrata's army finds its modern equivalent in a wave of strikes by women — not sex strikes (except by sex workers) but strikes in which women withdrew their labor, paid and unpaid, from the workforce and their homes. A Day Without a Woman was a strike action held on International Women's Day in 2017 in the United States in which women were urged not to go into work, not to spend money, and to wear red as a sign of solidarity. It intersected with similar actions worldwide that were held on the same day. Only a few thousand participated in the United States, but a year later, half a million women went on strike in Spain. A women's strike in Poland in 2016 resulted in the government reversing its plans to impose an absolute ban on abortion. As Cinzia Arruzza, Tithi Bhattacharya, and Nancy Fraser put it in their manifesto *Feminism for the 99%*, "a new feminist wave is reinventing the strike. . . . Breaking through the isolation of domestic and symbolic walls, the strikes demonstrate the enormous political potential of women's power: *the power of those whose paid and unpaid work sustains the world.*"[22]

A women's labor strike is less likely to spark hashtags and op-eds than a sex strike, but it is the best blueprint for political action offered by the Lysistrata myth.

THREE

DIETING WITH HIPPOCRATES

DIET BOOKS AND PLANS COME AND GO. FATS ARE IN, CARBS are out. Wellness is in, calorie counting is out. Fasting is in, keto is out. What remains consistent in these plans is their use of Hippocrates, the ancient Greek father of medicine, to promote dieting.

Among the books that used to be on my shelves, Hippocrates was quoted in *The 17 Day Diet*; *The Adrenal Reset Diet: Strategically Cycle Carbs and Proteins to Lose Weight, Balance Hormones, and Move from Stressed to Thriving*; *Flat Food, Flat Stomach: The Law of Subtraction*; *Fat Loss Factor*; and *Eat Right 4 Your Type: The Individualized Diet Solution to Staying Healthy, Living Longer and Achieving Your Ideal Weight*. Hippocrates also stars in Weight Watchers' online calendar of Motivational Weight Loss Quotes. The Weight Watchers calendar is typical of the careless way in which Hippocrates is often used. The motivational quotation for May 8 is "Extreme remedies are very appropriate for extreme diseases" (Hippocrates), an incentive that is both vague and alarming and that appears to be contradicted by the motivational quotation for May 9: "Everything in excess is opposed by nature" (Hippocrates).

Most commonly Hippocrates is used to illustrate the simple idea that being fat is very unhealthy for you. For example, in the book *Practical Paediatric Nutrition*, we are told that obesity is "perhaps the most obvious situation which provides a health risk and which may be present, and preventable, in childhood. 'Sudden death is more common in those who are naturally fat than in the lean' (Hippocrates)."[1] This is the most frequently quoted line from Hippocrates, and it is used to scaremonger: if you are fat you will die. It is a message that is consistent with our society's prevailing attitudes toward fatness, that it is something to be feared. We are urged to "make war on" obesity as if fat bodies pose an equivalent threat to ISIS and to "tackle" obesity like one might a home invader. This, of course, makes a fat person feel at war with, and on guard against, her own self and encourages her, and others, to treat her body like an enemy of the state, which might not be the healthiest way to live either, but more of that later.

Hippocrates may seem like a surprising authority for modern health writers. Medicine has come a long way since the fifth and fourth centuries BCE. You don't see modern doctors advocating his remedies in a hurry. His prescription for male pattern baldness was to apply to the head a mixture of opium, horseradish, pigeon shit, beetroot, and spices, and if that failed,

castration was a possible surgical solution. Nor, thank good-
ness, are his cures for the "diseases of virgins" all the rage in
today's pediatric medicine, advocating as they do that girls
should get married and have sex as soon as their menstrual
periods start, to avoid going mad.

Diets, however, are often sold by appealing to the authority
of the past: just as the paleo-diet craze seeks legitimation from
the Paleolithic era, diets that quote Hippocrates seek legitimation from his legendary status as the first Western doctor. This
itself is a bit of a fiction because Hippocrates cannot possi-
bly have written all the treatises that survive in the collection
known as the Hippocratic Corpus. There are more than sixty
of them, and they were written over a wide span of time—
when we talk about "Hippocrates," we mean him or one of
his associates.

Hippocrates would not have endorsed modern diet culture:
the restriction of calories in pursuit of a number on a scale and
our obsession with being slim. He did disapprove of gluttony:
the excessive and extravagant consumption of food, drink, and
other bodily pleasures; but gluttony was not typically associated with fatness by Hippocrates and other ancient writers. In
ancient Greece, fat in general terms often had positive connotations of richness, prosperity, and thriving, while thin often
suggested poverty and weakness. Some uncertainty is caused
by the difficulties of translating from ancient Greek into English. The Greek adjective *pachus*, which is often translated as
"fat," can also mean "stout" and "stocky." It could also suggest
heft, both physically and socially, which our word *fat* does not.

President Trump and former president Bill Clinton (before his weight loss) would likely have been called *pachus*.

In the Hippocratic Corpus, everyone's body is considered constitutionally different and shaped by a variety of factors: geography, environment, bodily humors, diet, and exercise. Crucial for good health is getting these things in the right balance, but the Hippocratic writings never state that if you are fat it is important for your health that you lose weight.[2] We are told that being fat could be detrimental to a woman's fertility, but then so could living in cities that were exposed to hot winds.[3] Hippocrates does give advice to people who are fat (or stocky) and who do want to lose weight: don't eat while exercising; eat before you have cooled down after exercising; drink tepid, diluted wine before exercising; eat one meal a day; stop bathing; eat rich, seasoned food so that you will more easily be satisfied; and sleep on a hard bed.[4] (I'm not sure about sleeping on a hard bed, but drinking wine before exercising makes me perk up when I contemplate a visit to 24 Hour Fitness.) When it comes to the body, *balance* is key for Hippocrates. What of the diet books' most frequently quoted line, "People who are naturally very fat are apt to die earlier than those who are thin"? This is one of Hippocrates's aphorisms and is sandwiched between an observation that individuals who have been hanged by the neck and are unconscious but not quite dead will not recover if they are foaming at the mouth and the opinion that epilepsy in young people is most frequently alleviated by "changes of air, of country, and of ways of life."[5]

There is no narrative context that expands upon and clarifies the saying. What's more, even the meaning of that brief line isn't quite clear. The Greek can mean that people who are naturally very fat will take less time to die, when they die, than people who are thin—not that they will die at a younger age or prematurely. We might think this is a *good thing*. The *Aphorisms* also contain other advice that is relevant to, but completely ignored by, modern diet gurus. Aphorism 1.5 advises against restrictive diets for healthy people (breaking such a diet was a risk to one's health), and aphorism 2.16 warns: "When in a state of hunger, one ought not to work hard." Hippocrates's outlook was considerably more complicated and varied than modern diet books that use him admit. When we select only quotations that may present fatness in a negative light, we distort the bigger picture in the Hippocratic Corpus and recruit Hippocrates as a spokesman against obesity, which he was not.

Why does it matter if diet peddlers misappropriate Hippocrates? I am not a purist or pedant when it comes to how we today understand and use antiquity. Misquoting ancient texts can be productive and creative.[6] The distortion of Hippocrates bothers me because his writings are being conscripted by the diet industry to promote misery and sickness. I have been teaching in universities in England and in the United States for over twenty years. In my experience one of the biggest challenges to female students' well-being, as great as exam stress and financial debts, is disordered eating.

When I had first started teaching at the University of Reading in England, one of my students, an intelligent, vibrant, lovely young woman, died from a heart attack brought on by chronic bulimia. Many other students with bulimia and anorexia have been unable to attend lectures regularly and their grades have suffered. Countless students (and colleagues) have confided that they are dissatisfied with their bodies. One of my female colleagues intermittently fasts, another rarely consumes anything when she's at work except for a fermented milk drink, and another will not eat dairy, grains, gluten, or sugar. Of course, men are affected by diet culture too. Even the Norse god Thor, in the movie *Avengers: Endgame*, cannot escape being shamed for having put on weight. However, he has not been reduced to marketing diet products as Wonder Woman has, with ThinkThin bars flashing from her bracelets; the message: dieting is empowerment. As Roxane Gay puts it, "The desire for weight loss is considered a default feature of womanhood";[7] in contrast, the desire for weight loss is not a default feature of manhood. The unhappiness caused by "normal" dieting and the mental real estate taken up by obsessing about food, is a staggering waste of our time, energy, and talent.

So why have I spent most of my life, since late childhood, on and off diets? It wasn't for health reasons, even though I sometimes said it was, because I'm in pretty good health. Nor was it to feel more attractive (when I have been slim, I haven't felt more attractive, but I have felt more accepted). I think it's been for two reasons. The first is that thinness connotes success in our culture, while fatness suggests failure: moral and intellectual laziness and lack of self-control. Academic life is fiercely competitive: I wanted to be *and look* successful. The second is that, whereas the research part of my job can be done in private with no one watching me (the philosopher Jacques Derrida famously wrote in his pajamas), lecturing is a different matter. The spotlight is, quite literally, on me, along with the judging eyes of students. Undergraduates can be merciless in their scrutiny and their scorn.

Academia, no less than the rest of society, is a world where stigma and shame around how you look is routine. The system of teaching evaluation questionnaires, the student feedback that plays a role in tenure and promotion evaluations, has recently come under attack for its gender and racial biases: studies have shown that students use different, and less positive, language for female professors and professors of color. Reading student questionnaires that comment on teachers' looks can, for the fat professor, feel like being trolled. Appraising a professor's appearance as well as their teaching was for many years encouraged and normalized by the popular website Rate My Professor, where students post public evaluations of their teachers, including, until 2018, "hotness" ratings: How many chili peppers did you get? Faculty also sit in judgment, though few are as overt in their contempt as the psychology professor at the University of New Mexico who, a few years ago, sent this tweet: "Dear obese PhD applicants: if you didn't have the willpower to stop eating carbs, you won't have the willpower to do a dissertation #truth."[8]

Would ancient Greece and Rome have been much more accepting of fat people than modern-day North America? It is difficult to know because respectable women's figures were not typically displayed and discussed. The images of people on vases were highly stylized, and weight per se was not a hot issue. Greek insistence on rigorous bodily discipline (athletics for men and, in Sparta, for women too) coupled with frugal food provision must have made fatness far less common than it is today. It is important to avoid the trap of romanticizing antiquity; there is no evidence that being fat was a mark of beauty in ancient Greece as it is in, say, modern Mauritania.

However, one good indication of attractiveness is provided in statues of Aphrodite (or Venus, as the Romans called her), goddess of love and lust. She is depicted in different sizes and poses. The statue type known as Crouching Aphrodite, thought to have originated in the third century BCE and frequently copied and adapted by Roman artists, shows the naked goddess in a crouching pose, her stomach folded into several rolls of flesh. Scholars tend to discuss statuary of the curvy female body in terms of "symbolizing fertility."[9] They might be right, but the language of fertility is rather clinical, reminiscent of ovulation charts and hormone injections. It might make us forget that Aphrodite is, above all else, *sexy*. Statues of Aphrodite and Venus were the epitome of gorgeousness in ancient Greece and Rome, but if they were brought to life today, they would be told to go on a diet.

These statues are a measure of how times, and beauty standards, have changed. Roughly a hundred years ago, liberal

If Aphrodite were alive today, she'd be told to go on a diet. (Crouching Aphrodite, second century CE.)

GETTY IMAGES / DEA / ARCHIVIO J. LANGE

arts colleges for women in the northeastern United States would host competitions to see which of their student bodies most closely resembled the statue known as the Venus de Milo. Wellesley College in Massachusetts took the measurements of all students individually, and then released the composite data on February 10, 1916. The data was used to boast about the beauty of Wellesley women: it was pointed out that the average student at the college had a waist circumference within half an inch of that of the Venus de Milo. Five days later, on its front page, the *Chicago Daily Tribune* reported that Wellesley's composite Venus was "outdone by Miss Margaret Willett, the beauty of Swarthmore college and leader in women's athletics, according to measurements of Miss Willett made public today by her friends." The article, titled "Best Wellesley Venuses: Swarthmore Girl Said by Those Who Measured Her to Have a Perfect Figure," goes on to explain: "In height, weight, and waist measurements the Swarthmore girl varies only by the smallest fraction of an inch from the Venus de Milo. The bust is practically the same and the leg measurements are almost identical."[10]

This was absurd. For starters, the notion that students weighed the same and had similar measurements, including height, as the Venus de Milo cannot be true. The Venus de Milo, as you can see if you visit her in the Louvre Museum in Paris, is 6 feet, 8 inches in height. I don't know what the statue weighs, but given that it is made from solid marble, a lot more than a college student. Unless Wellesley and Swarthmore students were as a community freakishly tall and heavy, while also having flat stomachs and modest busts, their measurements could not have been almost identical to the Venus de Milo. Miss Willett was reported to have been 132 pounds and 5 feet, 4.8 inches tall.[11] The likely explanation is that the students were measured against a plaster cast, or casts, of the Venus de Milo. We know that a cast of the Venus de Milo was among the replica antiquities that lined the hallways of Wellesley College, and other colleges had their own casts.[12] The realization that the aesthetic ideal for female students was *a cast* of the Venus de Milo reveals (one way in which) the exercise was ridiculous and undermines the futility of all that precise measuring. After all, casts come in a wide range of heights and weights.

And what is with the creepy practice of college faculty measuring students' bodies? This had been standard practice for women (and, to a lesser extent, men) in elite colleges since the 1890s, when physical educators like Dr. Dudley Allen Sargent, director of the Hemenway Gymnasium at Harvard University, collected measurement cards from students at a number of institutions for research purposes.[13] In 1893, Sargent used this data to design a statue based on composite figures from female students' measurements. It was exhibited at that year's Chicago World's Fair and became known as the Harvard Venus. Visitors to the fair were invited to compare their own bodies to the statue, thereby continuing the use of statues of Venus as a touchstone against which to measure real women's bodies, but with a twist: this statue was compiled using data about real women's bodies.

The creation of an image of ideal beauty from a composite of real women's bodies is a practice that goes back to the famous Greek artist Zeuxis, who lived during the fifth century BCE. One anecdote about him tells how, when he could not find one women beautiful enough to pose for a painting of Helen, the most beautiful woman in the world, he brought in five different women to model for him and painted Helen from a compilation of their best features.[14] Another anecdote tells how Zeuxis died. He was commissioned to do a painting of Aphrodite by an old (and presumably, according to the logic of the tale, unattractive) woman, who insisted on modeling for the painting herself. While attempting to do the painting, Zeuxis died laughing.[15] This anecdote pokes fun at Zeuxis and his "realistic" method of painting and at the relationship between model and subject. It also shows that mocking women who want to see themselves as beautiful has a very long history.

I wonder whether a student at Wellesley or Swarthmore or Harvard who had been born without her arms, or who had lost them later in life would have been held up as the perfect beauty.[16] The drive to idealize, seen in the practice of comparing women to the Venus de Milo, is so strong that it ignores or overlooks the fact that the statue is armless, due to damage it sustained before and after it was dug up in 1820. The famous statue *Alison Lapper Pregnant*, sculpted by Marc Quinn as a portrait of British artist Alison Lapper, who was born without arms, echoes the Venus de Milo and highlights how the ancient statue can be used as model for seeing beauty in disability and that perfection takes many forms.[17]

Much of Dr. Dudley Sargent's behavior is repellent to our sensibilities, but his choice of the Venus de Milo as an ideal paradigm for American womanhood was, in one important way, radical. It was a reaction against the feminine ideal in the Victorian period, when women wore corsets and dresses with bustles and so had tiny pinched-in waists and exaggerated hips and bottoms. In an article in *Harper's Bazar* in 1897 titled "Sorrows of the Fat," Edith Bigelow wrote about the "crime" and "deformity" of fatness. For Bigelow, Venus was not the ideal beauty but too chubby for the fashions of the day: "Venus herself couldn't fasten those bodices, and if she wore stays they would have to be made to order." She went on to say that only in the uncivilized world of Africa would large women be thought beautiful.[18] "Sorrows of the Fat" was part of a trend in the eighteenth and nineteenth centuries, in both scientific theories and popular culture, which linked fatness to blackness and thinness to whiteness. Sociologist Sabrina Strings has demonstrated that fat phobia in relation to black women did not stem from medical concerns about health but with the association during the Enlightenment era among fatness, blackness, stupidity, and savagery. Conversely, and at the same time, an association grew among thinness, whiteness, intelligence, and civilization. These images were, as Strings puts it, "used to degrade black women *and* discipline white women."[19]

Only after these racist and misogynist ideas had taken hold did medical writings use "science" to confirm the undesirability of being fat. This is another reason why quoting Hippocrates in modern diet books is misleading: it suggests that there is an unbroken line of medical approbation of fatness from antiquity to today and obscures the fact that attitudes toward body size are, and have been, about much more than medicine and health. The diet industry is built upon an ideology of racial, as well as gender, prejudice.[20]

My experience—as well as that of most men and women I know—has been that diets don't work. After every significant weight loss, I have gained it all back *and more*. I was first put on a diet when I was ten years old and my mother declared that my ass looked like a shelf. I was allowed one thousand calories per day, plus a bag of Maltesers chocolates as a treat every evening. If I allow myself to sink into the memory of it, I can still feel the desire I felt for those Maltesers, the shame of wanting them so desperately, the taste of the red crinkly paper as I licked it clean. I hadn't particularly bothered about Maltesers before, but rationing food made them all the more desirable. My story is not unusual. "Results not typical" declares every commercial lauding a celebrity's weight loss, and yet we still put our time, money, and faith into diets. We are told so frequently, and in so many different ways, that being fat equals being unhealthy, that the economic elements underpinning this belief remain concealed. Much modern "health" is driven by what is in the financial interests of pharmaceutical companies. One example: whether or not a person is overweight or obese is commonly determined by reference to the body mass index (BMI). The BMI was set using standards drawn up by the World Health Organization (WHO), which relied on recommendations from the International Obesity Task Force (IOTF). At the time, the two biggest funders of the IOTF were pharmaceutical companies that between them had a monopoly on selling weight-loss drugs. Go figure.

There is scientific evidence that doing regular exercise prolongs life but not that weight loss does so.[21] There is yet to be research carried out into the damage caused by doctors' prescribing diets, shaming fat patients, and misdiagnosing them because they don't look beyond their own assumptions about fat. Journalist Laura Fraser tells how her sister, Jan Fraser, died at the age of fifty-nine from endometrial cancer in 2016. Endometrial cancer is a relatively easy cancer to diagnose, but Jan's was overlooked. According to Jan, her ob-gyn could not see beyond her size: "He didn't do anything for me, and he didn't find anything. He just saw me as a fat, complaining, older woman."[22] In 2018, Ellen Bennett, another fat woman who died of cancer at a young age, used her own obituary to attack medical professionals for fat shaming rather than treating her: "Over the past few years of feeling unwell she sought out medical intervention and no one offered any support or suggestions beyond weight loss. Ellen's dying wish was that women of size make her death matter by advocating strongly for their health and not accepting that fat is the only relevant health issue."[23] My own grandmother, a hearty seventy-year-old with a zest for life, experienced similar treatment. She had a stomach ulcer that was not diagnosed. When she complained of pain, her doctor did not run tests but instead told her to lose weight. Her ulcer untreated, she died a painful and preventable death.

When it comes to fat people, the medical profession fails repeatedly to honor the Hippocratic oath, sworn by all physicians. Part of it is to "remember that I remain a member of society, with special obligations to *all* my fellow human beings" (my emphasis) and to abide by the maxim "first do no harm" (this is not, as is often thought, in the oath itself, but an equivalent sentiment is found in Hippocrates's *Epidemics*).[24]

Even when there's evidence that being fat in certain circumstances might be beneficial for health, it is explained away. Take one article, titled "Obesity and Cardiovascular Disease: Risk Factor, Paradox, and the Impact of Weight Loss," in the *Journal of the American College of Cardiology*.[25] The authors discuss numerous studies that document how overweight and obese people (their terminology) with established cardiovascular disease have a better prognosis compared with patients who are not overweight or obese. They call this the "obesity paradox," which is a pejorative formulation. It might more accurately be described as evidence that contradicts and complicates the mainstream scientific view that obesity is simply, always, and in every way bad for you. In a short section the authors discuss the correlation between high BMI and risk of stroke. They conclude the section by—and here, once again, rhetoric substitutes for analysis—quoting that overused line from Hippocrates: "Sudden death is more common in those who are naturally fat than in the lean." Later they make it clear that "mortality after gastric bypass has recently been reported to be higher than expected" (in other words, "sudden death is more common in those who have gastric bypass surgery") but conclude that this shouldn't get in the way of "purposeful weight reduction."

Relief from the misery of dieting came for me when I began to practice intuitive eating, an approach that teaches you how to create a healthy relationship with your food, mind, and body, through listening to yourself and your body's cues, not to medical experts.[26] Intuitive eating has two main tenets: you should honor your hunger by eating until you are full (the tricky bit here is to learn to distinguish between hunger and appetite), and if you do habitually eat until you feel overfull, you should examine why you do this and tackle the causes of emotional eating. These two principles resonate with the discussion of self-indulgence in the *Nicomachean Ethics*, a work by the philosopher Aristotle, who lived in the century after Hippocrates. I should emphasize that Aristotle's language is a far cry from that of intuitive eating, which stresses that you should be kind to yourself: he is strict about moderation and censorious about those who overindulge with eating and drinking (he calls them *gastrimargoi*, "gut-mad," and characterizes overeating as bestial). However, he is interested in the psychology of eating to excess.[27] We now know that there are many answers to why people habitually eat when we are no longer hungry: we use food to cope with overstimulation, to numb emotions, and to protect ourselves (a significant number of compulsive eaters are survivors of physical and sexual abuse).[28] Of course, Aristotle did not identify these, but in suggesting that we honor our hunger (no matter our size—he was not bothered by fatness) and in addressing the question of why we overeat, Aristotle may (with a bit of deliberate pressing and suppressing) prove a better path to modern health than Hippocrates.

Choosing which ancient thinkers to hold up as authorities in the modern world, and how we selectively interpret them, is a politicized business with real-life ramifications. Classical antiquity is sufficiently rich and varied to provide material that can counter the narratives that we have wrenched from, and built upon, it. Aristotle's call to eat until satiety and to reflect on the reasons for overeating is a better prescription for human happiness and health than Hippocrates's aphorism, hijacked by the diet industry to scare us all into starving, purging, and doing strange things with maple syrup and cayenne pepper. It is a recipe for approaching ourselves with kindness and curiosity—and that is a genuinely good thing.

FOUR

THE WOMEN CONTROLLERS

WHATEVER YOUR SIZE, YOU MUST BE CAREFUL, IF YOU ARE A schoolgirl, not to expose your body too much. What too much means is not determined by the weather, fashion, or the girl's comfort but dictated by the school dress code. When my daughter, Athena, was in middle school, the head of faculty, who was also the wife of the headmaster, told the girls that they could not have visible bra straps or exposed cleavage or wear short skirts because it was *distracting to the male teachers*. I'll just let that sink in. The wife of the headmaster told girls aged twelve years and above that their bra straps, cleavage, and thighs must be covered lest they distract her husband and his male colleagues. When the girls pointed out that this was creepy and inappropriate, they were told that the teacher had misspoken: what she had meant to say was that it would be "distracting to the academic environment." We now know what this phrase means.

Policing the dress of schoolgirls has become something of a moral panic. Few schools are as extreme as Lord Grey School in Buckinghamshire, England, which, on the first day of term, sent home seventy girls on the grounds that their skirts were too short or their pants too tight, but every day girls are "coded" for wearing clothing that, in the eyes of school administrators, is "distracting." According to the dress code at Athena's middle school, when it came to skirts and shorts, "the length must exceed the knuckle of the middle finger of the hand when the arms are extended down to the side." Cue arguments in the changing room of H&M over whether the shorts really did come down longer than the knuckle of her middle finger, or whether they only did when she lilted away from whichever side I was measuring in order to make the shorts seem longer.

If in doubt, the school handbook warned us that "the headmaster's judgment about the appropriateness of a student's appearance shall be final whether or not the apparel is described in the handbook or in the supplemental guidelines." The school imposed an adult perception of what was sexually exciting onto children. It allowed for the kind of authoritarian madness that led to Stephanie Hughes, a student at Woodford County High School in Kentucky, being sent home from school because her *collarbone* was showing. According to Stephanie's mother, the school had said that her daughter's collarbone might distract the male students.

Why the need for this obsessive monitoring of students' clothes? Girls' appearances are subjected to intense scrutiny. Boys as well as girls of color also have their clothing and hair policed. Many schools, including Athena's middle school, ban "extreme hairstyles such as dreadlocks," and African American and Native American children are routinely punished for wearing their hair in its natural texture or having braided extensions.[1] Where dress codes directly address boys' clothing, it is sagging pants and jewelry that are forbidden, supposedly in order to prevent gang activity, even though these styles have long been part of mainstream fashion. Latinx students and African American students are more likely to wear these fashions and therefore to violate the dress code.

Whatever purpose these dress codes serve, it is clearly not about "protecting the academic environment," whatever that phrase means. I have spent my adult life in academic environments, in the US and the UK, and they are not an endangered species. Nor do they all follow the same template. At Cambridge University, academics and students wear whatever they want. Leggings, jeans, and sweaters are more common than suits and ties, and students often dye or shave their hair. Few professors are renowned for their fashion sense, and on the rare occasion that the sun comes out, so do the Hawaiian shirts and sandals worn over socks. Presiding over formal events such as examinations or high table dinners might require academic gowns. These are long, black, cloak-like garments that are brilliant for covering up stains but which make professors look like a murder of demented crows. Amazingly, cutting-edge academic work still gets done.

At the University of California, Santa Barbara (UCSB), where I now teach, the professors tend to dress more smartly than those at Cambridge University, but most students dress for comfort. When the temperature hits 80 degrees, the campus resembles a spring break party. I found it perplexing how outfits that were banned at my daughter's middle school are commonplace in the university up the road. My lecture halls are a sea of spaghetti straps and short-shorts. Every day, students with exposed bra straps write brilliant papers on chemical engineering and computer science. Their fellow students and professors manage to discuss military history and analytic philosophy with these young women without losing their focus. Despite the ubiquity of exposed female collarbones, UCSB has six Nobel Prize winners. Academic environments are created by everyone coming together with a desire to learn and to teach, not by taking a tape measure to girls' skirts.

Dress codes are necessary, some educators argue, because girls' fashion has changed. Girls are sexualized by fashion in ways in which they were not in previous generations, encouraged by hypersexy pop stars, gyrating in music videos. High school principal Christine Handy-Collins observes that what is considered sexy today is different when she was growing up in the 1970s and 1980s: "You want to look good. You want to be fashionable. That's always been the case," she says. "But our mini[skirt] was different than their mini is."[2] Diane Levin author of *So Sexy, So Soon*, points the finger at the deregu-

lation of television in the 1980s, a change that made it legal
to promote toys to children that were linked to TV programs,
like Bratz dolls, whose doe eyes, plastic pouts, and micro-skirts
make Barbie look frumpy. A conspiracy, then, among Bratz,
Nicki Minaj, and Abercrombie & Fitch? Well, no. And not
just because this line of reasoning puts the blame, eventually,
on the girls, who, as consumers of pop culture and buyers of
fashion, are complicit in turning themselves, runs the argument, into distracting objects. But also because viewing dress
codes as a new phenomenon, as a twenty-first-century response
to female bodies, ignores the fact that policing women's dress
is not just a present-day practice. It has a long and ugly history.

Ancient Greek and Roman regulations are a small, but
foundational, part of the long history of dress codes.[3] At
its beginning are the *gunaikonomoi*, the "women controllers,"
of ancient Greece. *Gunaikonomoi* were city officials, elected to
office, whose responsibility was to ensure that women dressed
and behaved appropriately.[4] In most cities, respectable women
were not allowed out in public much; they spent their time in
the women's quarters of their homes. Slaves and poor women
would have been forced to venture out to get water or work.
The city of Sparta scandalized citizens of other Greek cities
by allowing its women to exercise in public training areas,
but by and large, the only time that respectable women went
out in public in ancient Greece was for religious festivals and

events like funerals and weddings. Even women's participation in the festivals was likely to have been determined by the women controllers, who, scholars believe, chose which girls and women were selected for coveted roles within festivals. For example, every year in Athens, two girls between the ages of seven and eleven years old were chosen to serve in the cult of Athena Polias (Athena in her role as patron goddess of the city), and then to play major roles in a festival honoring the goddess called the Arrhephoria. Women who had committed adultery were not allowed to participate in Athenian festivals or to enter temples, and it might have been the job of the *gunaikonomos* to keep records of women who had been found guilty of committing adultery and to enforce the law excluding them from public religious life.

Julius Pollux, a professor of rhetoric in Athens during the second century CE, defined the *gunaikonomos* as "an office concerned with orderliness of women." The Greek word that I have translated as "orderliness" is *kosmos*. It can mean the universe (order amid the chaos) and something well arranged or adorned: we get the English words *cosmos* and *cosmetics* from it. We find clues about these women controllers in three inscriptions from Pergamon and Smyrna (where the town of Bergama and city of Izmir in Turkey are now situated); they refer to an official, most probably the *gunaikonomos*, who was "the supervisor of decorum (*eukosmia*) for girls." *Eukosmia* means "good order" or "good adornment": the word has both connotations. Controlling adornment was inextricable from controlling order; dress and behavior were intimately associated.

It is difficult for us to work out exactly what the dress codes were, partly because our evidence is patchy, partly because different cities and festivals had different rules, and partly because much religious and cultic practice remains shrouded in mystery. One inscription (from Andania, a town in ancient Messenia, on the southwestern Peloponnese) bans gold accessories, blush makeup, hair bands, plaits, and all shoes except for ones made of felt or sacred leather. The woman's outfit as a whole was not allowed to be too expensive. Women of different statuses were given different spending limits: the sacred priestesses were allowed the highest limit of 200 drachmas, other girls 100 drachmas, and slave girls 50 drachmas. None of the women were allowed to wear more than two garments: a large cloak or wrap, called a *himation*, and a dress underneath it. Transparent clothing was explicitly forbidden. There were also rules about bands of color on the clothes, though precisely what the rules were is not clear. What is clear is that the women had to submit to clothing checks by the *gunaikonomoi*.

Various punishments are recorded for women who broke the dress codes or who were otherwise disorderly. The Andania inscription suggests that the *gunaikonomos* would tear the clothing that violated the dress code and dedicate it to the gods: "If any woman has her clothing otherwise, contrary to the decree, or some other prohibition, let not the *gynaikonomos* allow it, and let him have the power to tear it, and let it be dedicated to the gods." Did he do so on the spot, ripping the dress off the woman and publicly stripping her? We do not know for sure, but it is a distinct possibility. Even if the offending woman were allowed to go back home, change her clothes, and bring the garment back to the official for him to tear and dedicate to the gods, the dedication of the torn clothing would have been performed in a public place. The question is not whether the punishment was humiliating but to what extent. Elsewhere we read that girls and women who broke the dress code were given fines, and notices of their transgressions were posted on a white board on a plane tree in a public area; shaming was part of the penalty. Serious infractions of dress and behavior led to women being excluded from the religious life of the city for up to ten years. In other words, women who fell afoul of the women controllers could be put under a kind of house arrest, exiled from the few areas of public life that they were previously allowed to enjoy.

One of the most important pieces of evidence about the *gunaikonomoi* is Plutarch's *Life of Solon*, a book written in Greek during the Roman Empire, in which Plutarch describes a number of restrictions placed upon women in Athens by the lawmaker Solon, in the the early sixth century BCE. Several of these police women's clothing and behavior. When outside the house, we are told, women should not wear more than three outer garments. If they traveled at night, it had to be in a wagon with a lamp at the front, a rule presumably designed to prevent adulterous liaisons. Women's behavior at funerals was regulated; public displays of grief that were too passionate and prolonged were outlawed. Plutarch suggests that here men, too, were punished by the *gunaikomonoi* when they were excessively emotional and displayed what he terms "unmanly and womanish behavior."

Another source, from the third century BCE, quoted by a contemporary of Plutarch, tells us that in Syracuse, "the women should not wear golden ornaments, nor garments decorated with flowers, nor robes with purple borders, unless she professed herself to be a prostitute available to all."[5] Differentiating prostitutes from respectable women through dress codes was a practice that continued in the Roman Empire. At that time, prostitutes and adulterous women were designated *togata*, "toga wearing." Chaste women were labeled *stolata*, "dress wearing." The toga was the typical dress of the male citizen, or at least, the one who was wealthy enough to afford it. Unlike the typical depiction of togas today in fraternity parties and historical movies, in which the toga looks like a white bedsheet, togas in the Roman world were brightly colored, often saffron yellow.[6] In calling prostitutes and women who committed adultery toga wearers, Roman society marked out visibly and starkly girls and women who broke the sexual rules.

Before the scarlet letter came the yellow toga: some sources indicate that prostitutes and women who were found guilty of adultery were forced to wear togas. This dress code was imposed upon them as part of their punishment. Perhaps it shamed women whom society marked out as sexually transgressive by suggesting that they had the appetites of men and therefore had to dress as men. Certainly, the toga marked prostitutes out as public figures; respectable Roman women did not go out in public unattended, but prostitutes did, and making them wear the toga acknowledged their public presence in a way that was designed to humiliate them.

Scholars are not quite sure when the practice of electing women controllers ceased. The Roman politician Cicero, writing around 45 BCE during the Roman Republic, argued that the city of Rome should not elect them, though not because he was an early feminist: "And let us not set a prefect over women, in the fashion of the elected office among the Greeks, but let there be a censor, to teach husbands to control their wives."[7] In effect, Cicero argues for the privatization and domestication of the work of the women controllers. The election of state regulators may have stopped, but the practice of regulation continued.

On one remarkable occasion, women fought back against men controlling their dress and behavior. About 170 years before Cicero's discussion of the women controllers, a law was passed that forbade women to display more than half an ounce of gold (and so limited her ability to wear gold jewelry) and to wear multicolored (and therefore expensive) garments. It was known as the Oppian Law, and it was introduced in 216 BCE as an emergency measure, during wartime. There was a concern, during this period of austerity, that conspicuous displays of wealth would undermine traditional military values and encourage corruption.[8] But emergency measures are often used to impose greater social control, and scholars have suggested that the real reason for the legislation was to curb the increasing visibility and independence of Roman women.[9] Whether or not that was true, it is clear that the law was a means of policing Roman women's behavior and freedom of movement: it also forbade women to ride in a carriage in Rome or any city or town, except for the purpose of performing public religious rites. After the war had ended in a victory for Rome, there was pressure to repeal the law. One supporter of the law, Cato the Elder, spoke vehemently against women's freedom: "Our ancestors did not want women to conduct any—not even private—business without a guardian; they wanted them to be under the authority of parents, brothers, or husbands," he argued, castigating women's "unbridled nature," lack of self-control, and desire for freedom.[10] For days, the women of Rome protested, crowding the streets and blocking access to government buildings. The mass demonstrations were extraordinary—it was not socially sanctioned for women to assemble in public and protest—and they were successful: the Oppian Law was repealed in 195 BCE.[11]

Dress codes today are not always regulated by government officials as they were in antiquity, but they are still a way of controlling girls and making them feel ashamed of their bodies. They also inculcate conservative gender norms; school dress codes are used to stop boys from being too feminine, in a similar way to Plutarch's description of how the *gunaikonomoi* punished boys and men for "unmanly and womanish behavior." Dress codes consolidate cisgender differences; it is rare that boys are allowed to wear skirts or for any child to be allowed to cultivate a nonbinary gendered appearance. Racial hierarchies are maintained too, with students of color being policed and punished more frequently for dress code violations. School dress codes, like the Oppian Law in ancient Rome, are about more than dress: they are a means of enforcing patriarchal control. One might even conclude that they are *a pretext* for controlling girls, trans and gender nonconforming children, and students of color.

The stakes, for students who run afoul of dress codes, can be high. Deanna J. Glickman, assistant public defender in Robeson County, North Carolina, has argued that "dress codes serve as an entry point to the school to prison pipeline for trans students," as also they do, disproportionately, for students of color.[12] The school-to-prison pipeline funnels students who violate school rules straight into juvenile correctional facilities, criminalizing them and setting them up for failure. The latest available statistics show that girls of color are 2.8 times more likely than white girls to be suspended from school, often for minor infractions such as violating dress codes, and loss of school time has consequences for academic achievement, employment prospects, earnings potential, and health.[13] States that show greater racial bias in suspension rates (where girls of color are up to 5.5 times as likely to be suspended from school) are also states that have more stringent regulations around women's sexuality and reproductive rights. We can draw a line that connects the policing of girls' attire and a more systemic controlling of the rights of women, especially women of color.

School, after all, is where we first learn about the world and our place in it. Schools are teaching girls that their place is to be anxious and diminished. That girls' education is less important than that of boys, who need protecting from the danger of girls' bodies. That girls cannot be out in public without taking care that their appearance not distract and excite men. These ideas are nothing new. They underpin the assumption that when girls are sexually assaulted, they are to blame. *What was she wearing?* is the common response when girls are assaulted. Chanel Miller, the writer who was violated by the Stanford student Brock Turner was wearing a beige cardigan. You could be dressed in a hazmat suit, and some boys and men would still claim to be excited by what you are wearing.

Wearing the niqab, hijab, and burka does not protect women from harassment and assault. Shaista Gohir, chair of the Muslim Women's Network UK, which runs a helpline for Muslim women, told the *Independent* newspaper: "We receive calls on the helpline from Muslim women who disclose sexual assault and rape. They have been fully dressed. Some have been wearing a *hijab* (headscarf), *jilbab* (full robe), and even a *niqab* (face veil). The offenders have included family friends, family members, and also respected religious leaders in the community. Women's dress is an excuse popularized by men to justify their behavior so that they don't have to take responsibility."[14]

In ancient Rome, if a man sexually assaulted a woman who dressed as a prostitute, it was considered less of a crime than if he had attacked a woman dressed in the robes of a respectable woman. This legacy of what we now call slut shaming runs deep. Dress codes are repeatedly used as reasons for teachers to label girls as prostitutes and to blame girls for male sexual attention. One contributor to the Everyday Sexism Project, an initiative established to record instances of sexism experienced on a day-to-day basis, wrote, "I've been told by a teacher that the way I was wearing my socks made me look like a prostitute in my first year of school, making me 13, and I've been asked whether I'm ashamed of myself because I rolled my skirt up." The assistant principal of a North Dakota school explained that they had banned leggings and skinny jeans as "a way to prevent [girls] from distracting teachers and other students" and made the girls watch clips from the movie *Pretty Woman*, in which Julia Roberts plays a sex worker who is assaulted, to teach the girls about what clothes to avoid. The girls said it was like their teachers were, in effect, calling them prostitutes.[15]

Girls are categorized through their sexual availability to men, and clothing becomes a means of doing this. The myth that men and boys cannot control themselves from being "distracted" is one that we need urgently to challenge. What we call distraction is really male sexual aggression. We have bought the lie that says that men and boys cannot control being attracted to someone and cannot control their behavior when they are attracted to someone. The displaced aggression toward girls and women is evident in the rules and regulations about how they are to dress.

One school is challenging the assumption that male sexual aggression cannot be kept in check, or that men and boys can't learn how to treat women, trans, and gender nonconforming people with care and respect. Evanston Township High School in the Chicago suburbs has drawn up a dress code that prevents the shaming of students with as much energy as schools typically police errant bra straps. In 2018 it updated its dress code explicitly to forbid behavior and language that shames students: "Staff shall enforce the dress code consistently and in a manner that does not reinforce or increase marginalization or oppression of any group based on race, sex, gender identity, gender expression, sexual orientation, ethnicity, religion, cultural observance, household income or body type/size." It goes on to spell out that shaming includes the following:

- Kneeling or bending over to check attire fit
- Measuring straps or skirt length
- Asking students to account for their attire in the classroom or in hallways in front of others
- Calling out students in spaces, in hallways, or in classrooms about perceived dress code violations in front of others; in particular, directing students to correct sagged pants that do not expose the entire undergarment, or confronting students about visible bra straps, since visible waistbands and straps on undergarments are permitted
- Accusing students of "distracting" other students with their clothing[16]

So simple, so straightforward, yet in the current climate, downright revolutionary. Basic principles are listed, such as "certain body parts must be covered for all students at all times," and students are not allowed to wear anything that might be a safety hazard; that promotes hate speech, drugs, or alcohol; or that completely obscures the face (though hoodies and religious headwear are allowed).

The Evanston dress code shows that it is possible to change behavior and internalized values. It reminds children (and adults) that it is each person's responsibility not to be distracted by anyone else. Girls are not responsible for the way that boys respond to them. Or, in the words of the Evanston dress code: "All students and staff should understand that they are responsible for managing their own personal 'distractions' without regulating individual students' clothing/self expression."

There's a Greek myth that warns of the dangers, and the futility, of trying to control women. Its most famous version is the tragic drama *The Bacchae* by Euripides. The bacchae, also called bacchants or maenads, were female worshippers of the god Dionysus. The myth tells how Pentheus, the king of Thebes (whose name means "sorrow," which is a big hint right there) becomes enraged by the arrival from Asia of a new stranger, Dionysus, and refuses to acknowledge that he is a god. Dionysus is effeminate in his appearance (he is pansexual), which repels and fascinates the uptight Pentheus. In one production in 2008, Alan Cumming played Dionysus and entered the stage suspended upside down, with his bare butt showing under his gold lamé dress.[17]

GETTY IMAGES / PHAS

Trying to control women does not end well. (Pentheus about to be ripped apart by the bacchae, wall painting from Pompeii, first century CE.)

Under Dionysus's influence, the women of the city, including Pentheus's mother, Agave, have left their homes and are wandering round the countryside. Their appearance is shocking: they are dressed in fawn skins and wear their hair loose, with ivy and flowers in it. Pentheus is obsessed with regaining control of the women and vows that they "shall be hunted down out of the mountains like the animals they are."[18] He fantasizes about what the women are up to, now that they are no longer under the control of their men, and imagines them having orgies, when they are in fact doing nothing of the sort.

The wise prophet Teiresias warns Pentheus: "Do not be so certain that power is what matters in the life of man; do not mistake for wisdom the fantasies of your sick mind," but the king vows war on the women.[19] At this point, Dionysus, who has given Pentheus many chances to respect him, puts him in some sort of trance. He invites Pentheus to spy on the women in disguise, and the king dresses in women's clothes and a wig with long curls, posing and preening as he does so. Pentheus's ending is as gruesome and bloody as any in Greek myth: the bacchants, themselves under the spell of Dionysus, mistake him for an animal and rip him apart: "One tore off an arm, another a foot still warm in its shoe."[20] His mother rips off his head and impales it. And so the hunter becomes the hunted.

This is a myth that shows the dire consequences of hubris, of the arrogance of men who refuse to acknowledge and respect religion even if it is foreign to them. But it is also a cautionary tale about what happens when men try to control women. It ends up hurting them too. Every politician who argues for family values and then is caught in a sex scandal is a descendant of Pentheus. As is every educator who controls girls through dress codes because he cannot trust himself not to become distracted. I wish I had sent a copy of *The Bacchae* to Athena's middle school principal.

FIVE

#METU

DAPHNE, SO THE STORY GOES, WAS A WATER NYMPH WHO danced freely in fountains and across streams. One day, the god Apollo was seized with lust for her and pursued her when she rejected his advances and ran away from him. When she could run no longer, Daphne, terrified, cried out to her father, the river god, for help. He turned her into a laurel tree, saving her from sexual assault:

> *Her prayer scarce ended when heavy numbness seizes*
> *Her limbs, soft chest is walled with delicate bark,*
> *Hair grows into leafage, arms into branches,*
> *Feet once swift stick fast in motionless roots,*
> *Her face now a tree-top.*[1]

Thwarted, Apollo told her that he would plunder her branches and trunk to make musical instruments for himself to play on and arrows to shoot. He would pluck her leaves to weave them into wreaths for the victors of athletic competitions to wear. For Daphne, there was no escape from Apollo's physical violence after all.

Ancient myth dramatizes sexual assault again and again. These myths have become a valued part of our culture. Go into any major art museum and you will see Daphne metamorphosing into a tree alongside artworks such as *The Rape of Europa*, *The Rape of the Sabine Women*, *The Rape of the Daughters of Leucippus*, *The Rape of Philomela*, *The Rape of Proserpina*—the rape of Lucretia, Leda, Polyxena, Cassandra, Deianeira. . . . There are more paintings displayed in art museums in Europe and North America that feature a mythological rape scene than there are paintings displayed by female artists of color. Look up into the night sky and you will see ancient rape scenes emblazoned there too: Jupiter's Galilean moons are named for his victims Io, Europa, Ganymede, and Callisto.[2]

The myths provide us with a repertoire of rape narratives: ideas and beliefs that inform our own perspectives on sexual violence. The myth of Phaedra, who falsely accused her stepson of rape, tells us that women lie about being raped. The myth of Cassandra, who agreed to have sex with Apollo but then changed her mind and was punished with the "gift" that she would always speak the truth but would never be believed, tells us that women will be punished if we refuse to have sex and that no one will believe us when we tell the truth about having been assaulted. Medusa was a beautiful woman who was raped by the god Neptune in the temple of the goddess

Minerva. Minerva, insulted by the sexual activity in her sacred space, punished Medusa (but not Neptune) by turning her into a monstrous, snaky-haired Gorgon whose gaze turned men into stone. Her myth tells us that it is the raped woman who will be punished, not the rapist. Daphne called out to her father for help to escape Apollo's pursuit. More specifically, in a version by the Roman poet Ovid, Daphne asked him to destroy her beauty, which had "made her too pleasing."[3] The myth of Daphne's attempted rape tells us that it is the woman's appearance that is to blame for inciting male sexual aggression: she was asking for it.

The myth of Helen is perhaps the most dangerous of all the rape myths. Told and retold in different ways, some saying that Paris abducted her, others that she seduced Paris, the myths suggests that we will never be able to tell whether she was raped or whether she was willing.[4] These ideas about rape have been pernicious and persistent. They underpin the disbelief that met Christine Blasey Ford's testimony that Brett Kavanaugh attempted to rape her when she was fifteen years old, or the disbelief that she remembered accurately who her assailant was, even if she was indeed assaulted by someone (which is another way of not believing a woman, just with slightly more sophisticated rhetoric). All of these "lessons" about rape are firmly entrenched in our culture and must partly be responsible for the staggering underreporting of sex crimes to the police and the even more depressing conviction rates.[5]

Daphne, Medusa, Cassandra, and the other women and female spirits who are harassed and assaulted throughout Greek and Roman myth are not given crossover stories, like the super-heroes in the Marvel Avengers universe. They are never allowed to meet up and compare notes about their experiences or take collective action and call out the men and gods who have victimized them. Myth here does the work of an abusive partner: it isolates the women. They are never given a #MeToo moment.

Some argue that these narratives should not be read today. Ovid's *Metamorphoses* (written around 8 CE) has been particularly controversial; in some universities, students have demanded that it be removed from university curricula.[6] A long and influential Latin poem that tells stories of change (changing shape, changing bodies, changing sex), *Metamorphoses* features many descriptions of assault and has been criticized, with some justification, for eroticizing trauma.[7] So why should we read these myths? What do they have to tell us in the age of #MeToo?

Tarana Burke, the activist who founded #MeToo in 2006 as a grassroots protest movement to support women of color who had experienced sexual abuse before it became a global campaign in 2017 against sexual harassment, said that her key goal was to promote "empowerment through empathy." Some myths of sexual violence told by Ovid and other writers do just that. They invite us to empathize with the women who are assaulted, and they show insight into the psychology of sexual assault and the effects of trauma on the victims of the assault.[8]

Again and again, Ovid depicts women who are attacked leaving their bodies and turning into trees or bushes or clumps of reeds. I read these as imaginative dramatizations of the paralysis and dissociation caused by trauma. Daphne's response to Apollo's assault—she is unable to run or speak and a "heavy numbness seizes her limbs"—captures what happens to victims of sexual assault. Dissociation allows the person under attack to avoid experiencing the assault. Our rather stiff medical vocabulary terms this involuntary temporary paralysis *tonic immobility*. The feeling of leaving one's body and being alienated from it are well documented, as are their longer-lasting effects.[9]

I was assaulted when I was a young girl. Well into my adulthood, I had very little sense of my body. I was so disconnected from it that it was little more than a vehicle that carried my head around from place to place, from my neck to my knees could just as well have been made of wood. I read Ovid's *Metamorphoses* when I was thirteen and became fascinated by the story of Philomela and Procne.[10] Philomela was a young woman traveling to visit her sister Procne, who had recently married Tereus, the king of Thrace. Tereus accompanied Philomela from her home to his, but before they reached the palace, he brutally raped her. She cried out to the gods for help, but no one listened. When she threatened to tell the world what he had done, he cut out her tongue. He locked Philomela in a hut and told his wife that her sister had died during the journey. While Procne mourned, Philomela began to weave. She embroidered the whole story on a cloth (it took her a year) and sent it to her sister. Philomela had worried that her sister might consider her a rival and turn against her, but Procne's reaction was rage toward her husband.

Now, as an adult, I wince at the lingering description of Tereus's rape of Philomela, who is compared to a frightened lamb and a dove smeared with blood, "pale and trembling and all alone," and even more at the horrific account of how Tereus cut out her tongue with pincers and how the severed tongue twitches and murmurs on the ground. My professorial self cannot help notice that Ovid gives us little insight into Tereus's motivations or, more broadly, why men rape. We are just told that as soon as he saw her, "Tereus was inflamed, fast as ripened grain set alight or leaves, or hay stored in a barn put to the flame."[11] It is a common motif in ancient myth and one that allows men not to take responsibility for their actions: How can they be held accountable when they become so quickly aroused? Ovid also suggests that Tereus behaved the way he did in part because he was Thracian, a nasty bit of ethnic stereotyping.

But these were not the parts of the story that gripped my teenage self: I was obsessed with Philomela's determination to tell her story, with the fact that her sister believed her when she did so, and with Procne's brilliant, baroque, and hideous revenge on her rapist husband, even at great cost to herself. Revenge fantasies in ancient myths are not scripts to be followed, but they are adrenaline shots for the hurt soul, an essential part of the sexual assault survivor's emergency kit.

It is a gory tale, even by the standards of ancient myth. When she had read Philomela's tapestry and understood what her husband had done, Procne went to rescue her sister. That night happened to be the occasion of a festival in honor of Dionysus, which gave Procne a legitimate reason to leave the house. She dressed herself in the fawn skin and ivy costume of a bacchant, which was in keeping with her alibi but also an ominous sign of the uncontrollable anger that churned inside her.

After freeing Philomela, Procne devised a terrible means of retribution. She and Philomela slaughtered Procne and Tereus's young son, Itys, even as the child pleaded "Mother! Mother!" and tried to hug her. The sisters then cut up the boy's body "still warm and quivering with life" (a description that reminds us of Philomela's severed tongue), cooked it, and invited Tereus to dinner. Tereus "gorges himself with his own flesh and blood," and when he asks where his son is, Philomela brings in Itys's head and throws it in his face. There are striking echoes of *The Bacchae* here, but unlike Pentheus's mother, Agave, Procne and Philomela are not delusional: they know all too well what they are doing. We are also reminded of the myth of Medea, who killed her sons as revenge on her husband, Jason, who abandoned her and married another woman. The sisters are likened to Furies, primordial agents of revenge: female monsters, with snaky hair and eyes that drip gore. Ovid is as extravagant in his references to revenge myths, as Procne and Philomela are with their cannibal banquet.

Tereus lunges at the sisters with his sword, and as they flee him, all three of them turn into birds: Procne becomes a nightingale, Philomela a swallow, and Tereus a hoopoë or a hawk.[12] I used to think that the women's metamorphoses gave

71

them a happy ending, of sorts: they were free at last, literally "free as birds." However, there's another more sinister possibility, one suggested by horror movies in which humans are turned into animals: Philomela and Procne are trapped in the bodies of birds but with a human consciousness, doomed for the rest of their lives to grieve for Itys (*itys-itys* is said to sound like the cry of the nightingale) and to be pursued by Tereus, now a bird of prey.

Predatory men still silence women; the removal of Philomela's tongue was the original nondisclosure agreement.[13]At its core, the myth of Procne and Philomela is a myth about the refusal of a rape survivor to be silenced and the ability of women to take down abusive and powerful men, when they work together to do so. Procne could have chosen to side with her husband and to keep her son and all the social advantages of being queen. Instead, she chose to support her sister, at great cost to herself. She chose rage.

Philomela's cunning strategy for telling her story by weaving it into a tapestry is part of a larger cultural phenomenon in which women turn to weaving and craftwork as a means of resistance. It goes back to Homer's *Odyssey*, where we find Penelope besieged by suitors in her husband's long absence. She manages to avoid marrying one of them by a famous ruse. She promises to choose a new husband when she has finished her weaving; she weaves hard by day, but secretly undoes the work by night. And it looks forward to the radical textiles of British artist Tracey Emin and Egyptian American artist Shada Amer, and the pussy hats worn on the Women's March in 2017 by protestors of the inauguration of a president who boasted that women let him "grab them by the pussy."[14] Like Philomela's tapestry, the pussy hats made sexual assault visible through craft and (with some controversy) brought women together in protest.[15]

Other ancient myths about rape also focus on the impact of the crime on other women, something to which we today often turn a blind eye. One tells of the abduction of Proserpina (whose Greek name is Persephone), the young daughter of Ceres (Demeter), the goddess of agriculture, by Dis (Hades), the god of the underworld. In Ovid's telling of the story, a water nymph named Cyane tries to stop the god from taking her: "You'll go no further," she says. "You can't be Ceres' son-in-law against her will. Her daughter should have been courted, not raped."[16] As she speaks, she stretches out both her arms and tries to block the god's way. In fury, Dis strikes the pool and splits open the earth at its bottom, opening up a path to the underworld, where he disappears with Proserpina. Cyane, "mourning the goddess's rape and her own spring's violation, nurses in her heart a wound inconsolable."[17] In a metaphor that captures the slow enervation of grief, Cyane physically collapses and melts, until eventually she herself turns into water.

Proserpina's mother, Ceres, is so demented with grief that she is unable to tend to the harvests and plunges the world into famine. It is a well-known part of the myth that Proserpina is eventually reunited with her mother for six months of the year, but less well known is an episode before that, when

Ceres is wandering the earth searching for her daughter in the guise of a human being. She has given up hope and is incapacitated with despair when an old woman named Iambe makes her laugh by telling her a dirty joke.[18] This life-affirming moment pulls Ceres out of her grief and enables her to go on looking for, and eventually find, her daughter. This is another moment of female solidarity, when a woman's support changes the narrative of what happens in the aftermath of a rape.

Even in our post-#MeToo world, these myths can still resonate, as they did for me when I first read them. They are perceptive about the psychology of trauma, highlight victims' strength and strategies of survival, and guide our attention toward aspects of the experience of sexual assault that are sometimes overlooked. They also offer hints of women's empathy toward one another and the empowerment possible through those seemingly tiny moments of solidarity: a shared bawdy joke, the whisper network in the form of a woven cloth, and a selfless attempt to stop an assault.

I have been discussing these myths as if they mean the same today as they did in ancient Greece or ancient Rome. In part, they do: that is the power of myth. But in the case of Ovid's mythological stories, it is important to remember when and why he was writing about sexual violence. This was during the reign of the emperor Augustus, who imposed strict moral laws upon Rome. It was an oppressive and authoritarian regime, at least for a subversive writer like Ovid. There is a subtext to many of Ovid's stories about rape. The emperor frequently associated himself with the gods Jupiter and Apollo; in statues, on coins, and in cult, Augustus enhanced his image by connecting himself with them. The point of this was to present Augustus as powerful, as having divine imprimatur for his policies, and as sharing in the charisma of the gods. However, Ovid takes the association between the gods and emperor and uses it to reveal a different side of Augustus. Rather than focusing on the positive aspects of Jupiter and Apollo, Ovid represents them as repeatedly imposing their power upon unwilling victims. By association, he suggests that Augustus is autocratic and abusive. It is an effective technique. It gives Ovid an out: he avoids direct criticism of an emperor who was prone to exiling his opponents (and who did, eventually, exile Ovid) but allowed readers at the time to join up the dots and make the connection between Augustus and the rapist gods.

Let us join up our own dots in modern times by fast-forwarding from Ovid's Rome to today's Manhattan, more specifically to President Trump's penthouse on the sixty-sixth floor of Trump Tower on Fifth Avenue. Photographs published a few years ago gave us a rare glimpse into one of the president's homes.[19] The opulent interior of the penthouse features striking motifs from classical art and architecture (the designer was reportedly influenced by the Palace of Versailles[20]). There are marble Corinthian columns topped with gold, Greek vases (or replicas of them), classicizing statues, and, on the ceilings, painted murals. A painting above a marble mantelpiece depicts Apollo with Aurora, the Roman goddess of the dawn. It is clearly not a random choice. There is another image of Apollo on one of the ceilings: he is riding his sun chariot across the sky. It is hard to tell from the photographs, but it looks as if, in this painting, Apollo is wearing a laurel wreath. The *Daily Mail* newspaper, which published the photographs, said that the décor suggests "Trump sees himself in the mold of Apollo, Zeus's son and one of the most powerful of the gods." That may be so. But what does it mean for *us* to see him in the mold of Apollo? Can we avoid seeing less favorable associations between the president who jokes about grabbing women "by the pussy" and the god who attacked Daphne?

In some versions of the myth of Daphne and Apollo, it is not her father whom Daphne calls on to save her but Earth herself. The earth is personified as female in ancient myth: the Greeks called her Gaia, and the Romans knew her as Tellus Mater or Terra Mater: Mother Earth. One of the earliest accounts of the birth of the creation of the universe, *Theogony* by Hesiod (composed between the eighth and seventh centuries BCE), "broad-bosomed" Gaia was one of the first beings to exist. She gave birth to Uranus, the sky, "to be an equal to herself" and to be a place of safety for the gods. She joined with Uranus and bore many children, including the race of the one-eyed Cyclopes, the ocean, and a scheming son called

Cronus. Gaia and Uranus also produced three monsters who had one hundred hands and who were extraordinarily strong and violent. Hating them, Uranus hid them in secret hiding places within Gaia, a kind of assault upon Gaia, who was pained by his "shameful acts." Gaia plotted retribution: she fashioned a mighty sickle and incited her children to use it against their father. Cronus did so and castrated Uranus with the sickle. Right at the very beginning of the universe, and of recorded mythmaking, the earth was represented as female, as a mother, and as betrayed and injured by her lover in a shameful way.

We still use the language of personification and feminization to represent the earth, and we talk about the destruction of the earth in terms of rape: "the rape of the environment," "the rape of Mother Earth," "despoiling virgin forests."[21] These metaphors serve to reinforce humanity's dominance over the earth and diminish the importance of environmental concerns. After all, if mothers are routinely undervalued and women who have been raped are discredited and disparaged, then, by association through this figurative language, the earth and environment will be undervalued, discredited, and disparaged too.[22] In turn, when women are viewed as closer to nature, we are seen as less civilized, less fully human even, than men.

The myth of Daphne illustrates how the association of women with nature can demean both. When Daphne was turned into a tree, she escaped being raped by Apollo because the loss of her body made rape impossible. But as a tree she was no less an object for his use than when she was a woman (or, rather, a water nymph). After her metamorphosis, Daphne retained some of her humanness in her new being as a tree. Daphne had asked for her beauty to be destroyed, but after she was changed into a tree, we are told, her beauty remained. Apollo embraced and kissed the trunk and branches ("the wood shrank from his kisses"), and he felt her heart still beating under the bark. He told Daphne about what he planned to do with her: she would always be with him, as a wreath in his hair, as the wood in his arrows and his lyre. He told her that, through wreaths made from her laurel leaves, the Romans would proclaim the military triumphs of the emperor Augustus. Daphne was to become a symbol that celebrated Roman imperialism and, through the myth of the origins of the laurel wreath, a symbol that fused together imperialism and the victories of male over female and culture over nature. The final detail in Ovid's telling of the myth gives it a vicious twist. In response to Apollo's words, "the laurel nodded assent with new-made boughs and seemed to move its top like a head."[23] Daphne is made to betray herself and becomes complicit in her own devastation.

In another myth from Ovid's *Metamorphoses*, the tree, and the nymph inside it, get their revenge. This myth features another out-of-control king, and it is a cautionary tale about the consequences of sexually exploiting women and destroying the environment. This is the story of King Erysichthon of Thessaly, and if Erysichthon is too much of a mouthful, you could call him Earth-Ripper. It is what the Greek name means, and it is prophetic. King Erysichthon desired to build a banqueting hall. To clear space for it, he ordered that all the trees in the sacred grove to Ceres be cut down. When his workmen refused, Erysichthon seized an axe and he himself chopped the first tree down, killing the nymph inside. She cursed him with her dying breath. Ceres heard the nymph's curse and placed the spirit of insatiable hunger inside the king. The more he ate, the more ravenous he became. When his wealth had run out, he sold his daughter to get the money to buy food. He ate all the food in the land, all the crops and the animals, and he was still gnawed by hunger. Eventually, he devoured himself, limb by limb.

Even before capitalism, writers and mythmakers recognized that the biggest threat to global well-being is not poor people desperate to survive (welfare recipients, refugees, and economic migrants) but rich people desperate for more wealth. The myth of Erysichthon is an allegory for climate change,[24] and it makes a connection between the abuse of the environment and the abuse of women.

When the king sold his daughter, Mestra, in his greedy quest for wealth, he would have known that her master had the legal right to rape her and to prostitute her to others; she was his property. Mestra, however, was resourceful (she would go on to marry a thief named Autolycus, and together they would become the grandparents of the equally quick-witted hero Odysseus). She prays to the god Neptune to save her from slavery and implies that the god owes her a favor because he had previously "stolen her virginity" (she

Greed, destroying the environment, and prostituting women lead to catastrophe. (*Erysichthon Sells His Daughter Mestra*, Jan Havicksz, 1660.)

appeals, in other words, to her former rapist to save her from her future rapist). Neptune obliges and changes her into a fisherman, thereby confusing her new owner and allowing her to escape. Her father, however, exploits her new ability to change her shape and continues to sell her to "many masters" until the cash that he makes from this is useless because he has eaten all the food that money can buy. In the end, the king, in selling his daughter and consuming himself, destroys his future.

We know that cutting down trees in the Amazon rain forest results in multiple cascading effects: rain systems are weakened, forests die through lack of rain, and water supplies for cities like São Paulo and the crops that feed them are reduced.[25] We trust our politicians not to behave like King Erysichthon, but clearly our trust is misplaced because deforestation of the Amazon is increasing, not decreasing.[26] The effects of climate change are dramatically affecting the communities where we live. In December 2017, a wildfire named the Thomas Fire set ablaze Santa Barbara and Ventura Counties in California. Climate change is making wildfires more extreme and more damaging.[27] It took firefighters over two months to extinguish the Thomas Fire, by which time the fire had destroyed an area larger than the state of Iowa.[28]

I was not in Santa Barbara at the time; a few days before the fire started, I had left for England, where my mother was dying of lung cancer. As I watched my mother struggle for breath in a hospital room whose polystyrene ceilings were too low and lights too bright, I looked at videos taken by Athena from our apartment of a wall of fire advancing toward the city, while ash fell steadily and quietly: a parody of a white Christmas. My mum held on for a month, determined to make it to Christmas. I am grateful that I had time to say good-bye to her. Soon after I returned home, others in our neighborhood were not so lucky. The fire had burned down the trees whose roots are essential for holding the soil together. An intense rainstorm led to mudslides, although *mudslide* is too mild a term for what is really a tsunami of mud and boulders and debris. This mudslide killed twenty-seven people, suddenly and brutally, with no time for their loved ones to say good-bye.

Social justice activism that does not put the climate emergency at the top of its agenda will fail. There is no point in achieving equal pay if your workplace is being burned to the ground, and there is no point fighting for the rights of our daughters to have control over their bodies, if those bodies are being poisoned by a lack of clean drinking water. The specific practical solutions that we need to implement to prevent environmental disaster (if it is not already too late) are diverse and complicated. But the starting point is simple, and as ancient myth reminds us, it is also where we must start if we are to eradicate sexual assault. We begin by connecting with other people and with animals, trees, and the planet that we all live on, seeing them not as objects to be used but as living beings whose well-being is essential for us all to thrive. This is how we ensure that the final word of Ovid's *Metamorphoses* becomes prophetic for all of us—for the trees, plants, and animals and for the earth. *Vivam*: I will live.

SIX

DIANA, THE HUNTER
OF BUS DRIVERS

THE ROMAN GODDESS DIANA, WHOM THE GREEKS CALLED
Artemis, was a protector of girls and women. She saved Atalanta, when Atalanta's father wanted a son, not a daughter,
and so left his baby girl on a mountainside to be eaten by wild
animals or die from cold and hunger. She saved her hunting
companion Arethusa, who, like Diana, was committed to
remaining unmarried, from being raped by the river god Al-
pheus. And she saved many women in antiquity from death in
childbirth, and so, although Diana was a virgin goddess, the
Greeks and Romans believed she had a special role looking
after women in childbirth.[1]

Myth tells us that Diana and her twin brother, Apollo, were
born to Jupiter, king of the gods, and a goddess called Leto.
When Juno, Jupiter's wife, discovered her husband's infidelity

with Leto, she punished Leto by making it impossible for her to give birth on land. Leto suffered an unnaturally long and painful labor (in one account nine days and nights—can you imagine?), until she came upon an island that was floating and not connected to the ocean floor. As this was technically not land, Leto was finally able to give birth.[2]

Diana sat on her father's knee and asked for permission never to marry, to have a bow and arrow as her special weapons, to roam the mountainsides with her girl companions, hunting, and to be able to help women in childbirth.[3] The goddess was typically represented in her hunting gear, wearing a tunic and boots and carrying her bow and quiver of arrows. She looked a bit like Katniss Everdeen, the heroine of *The Hunger Games*, another protector of girls and a character modeled, in part at least, on Diana.[4] Men who intruded into Diana's world were swiftly punished, as the hunter Actaeon discovered. Actaeon stumbled upon Diana while she was naked, bathing in a pool in the forest. The goddess turned him into a stag, and Actaeon was ripped apart by his own hunting dogs.[5]

In 2013, many centuries after the dominion of the ancient Greek and Roman gods, another Diana emerged, in the border town of Ciudad Juárez, Mexico. She too was a protector of women and girls, and she too proved deadly to men. She presented herself as a version of the ancient Roman goddess. She is La Diana, la Cazadora de Choferes, or Diana, the Hunter of Bus Drivers.

This Diana killed with a handgun, not a bow and arrow. According to eyewitness reports, on the morning of August 28,

2013, a woman hailed bus number 718, climbed the steps, drew a gun, and shot the bus driver. He tried to escape but died on the sidewalk. Witnesses described the killer as a middle-aged woman with dyed blonde hair, or perhaps a blonde wig, wearing a cap, plaid shirt, and jeans. She killed again the following day, on the same bus route. This time she shot the driver while exiting the bus. She said something in his ear—witnesses say it was "You guys think you're real bad, don't you?"—and then shot him twice in the head.

One day later, local news stations received an email:

You think that because we are women we are weak, and that may be true but only up to a point, because even though we have nobody to defend us and we have to work long hours until late into the night to earn a living for our families we can no longer be silent in the face of these acts that enrage us. We were victims of sexual violence from bus drivers working the maquila shifts [shifts at factories that make goods cheaply for export to the US] here in Juárez, and although a lot of people know about the things we've suffered, nobody defends us nor does anything to protect us. That's why I am an instrument that will take revenge for many women. For we are seen as weak, but in reality we are not. We are brave. And if we don't get respect, we will earn that respect with our own hands. We the women of Juárez are strong.

It was signed Diana, the Hunter of Bus Drivers.

The letter is an explanation, a defense, a warning, and a declaration of war. Diana presents herself as "an instrument" working on behalf of the city's women. She speaks as their collective voice: "We have nobody to defend us . . . we can no longer be silent . . . we were victims of sexual violence . . . we are brave . . . we are strong."

Juárez is a city that remains vibrant and resilient despite the problems of drug cartels, economic suffering exacerbated by NAFTA, and police corruption. Among the criminal acts perpetrated in the city, sexual violence toward women and the torture, abduction, and murder of women stand out. Accurate statistics are hard to get, but the NGO Red Mesa de Mujeres reports that from 1993 to 2017 more than 1,600 women were murdered in the city.[6] Bus drivers were accused of several rapes and murders of women who rode home after working late at night in the city's factories (*maquilas*).[7] The extent of their guilt is difficult to know for sure; some of their confessions were extracted under police torture.[8] Yuri Herrera, a journalist who investigated the killings by Diana in 2013, wrote: "There is a sense among the general population that buses are a bad place to be by yourself. Just this week a bus driver was arrested for allegedly raping a girl on her way to school." He interviewed a local woman, called Laura, who told him, "I remember when I was in high school I would hear a lot about it. My friends would say to me if you're going on the route, and no one's there, take a pen with you with the point facing outward, because you never know. That's been happening for years, years. And it's the same for the ladies working in the maquilas."[9] For these women, bus driver meant rapist. In making bus drivers the targets of her vigilante killings, Diana was not just avenging the sexual violence that a bus driver had committed against her. Symbolically, she was waging war on all of the city's rapists.

Despite a major police investigation, and the chaos that ensued for a time when bus drivers refused to go to work, Diana has never been caught. She vanished into the shadows.

Diana, the Hunter of Bus Drivers modeled her persona not on the Roman goddess Diana in general but on a specific statue of her that has become part of the national identity of Mexico. This statue, known as *La Diana Cazadora* (Diana, the Hunter), is a major landmark in Mexico City. It is located on Paseo de la Reforma, one of the city's largest and most important avenues. First put on display in 1938, this bronze Diana, naked and kneeling on one knee, strings her bow with an invisible arrow and aims it high into the sky.

La Diana stands a short distance from another statue, the golden *Angel of Independence*. The *Angel* was commissioned in 1900 to commemorate Mexico's War of Independence.[10] On top of a column blazes a golden statue of the Greek goddess Nike, goddess of victory, holding a laurel wreath and a broken chain to symbolize freedom; this was a common image of republican liberty during the nineteenth century. Together, the *Angel* and *La Diana* are protective icons of Mexico City. *La Diana* is so iconic a symbol that a model of it is on display at the National Palace in Mexico City, and replicas of the statue have been set up in other cities in Mexico, including Juárez.

Diana, the Hunter protects Mexico City. (*La Diana Cazadora* above a fountain in a roundabout on Paseo de la Reforma.)

The version in Juárez is glitzier than the original. It stands outside a restaurant (called La Diana), in front of a mirrored backdrop that both magnifies the glare (this replica is golden, not bronze) and the nudity of the goddess. The nudity has long sparked controversy. For twenty-five years, *La Diana* in Mexico City was given a loincloth to wear, after her nakedness allegedly offended the first lady and the Catholic Church. It was removed just before the Mexico City Olympics in 1968.[11] Further scandal came in 1992 when it was revealed that the model for the statue had been a sixteen-year-old girl, Verdayes

Helvia Martinez, who had requested, for the sake of her reputation, that her identity be kept anonymous.[12] But, if we remember the original myth, the most disconcerting aspect of the nudity of Diana is that it makes Actaeons of us all. Like Actaeon, we risk punishment if we see Diana naked.

The sculptor of *La Diana*, Juan Olaguíbel, confessed that, during the process, he had second thoughts about representing a figure from classical antiquity. The title that he eventually gave the statue was *La Flechadora de la Estrella del Norte* (The Archer of the North Star): she was an image of aspiration and inspiration, of shooting for the stars. For Olaguíbel, it was important that the archer represented Mexican beauty and not a classicizing (European) ideal. "I did not make a Diana the huntress," he said. "It is true that in the beginning this was my intention, but I resisted the classical beauty of the Greeks and decided to focus my attention on the Creole beauty of our women, and I sought as a symbol the arrow pointed heavenward. My statue is thus, *The Archer*, and nothing more."[13] The public had other ideas: they call her *La Diana Cazadora*.

I reflected on the meanings of statues, how those meanings come about, and on the subtle politics of protest, while walking through the leafy shade of Alameda Central, the large public park in Mexico City, with my partner and daughter. We were spending a long weekend in the city to look at the

La Diana statue and get a sense of its context within public art there. Alameda Central, named for the poplar trees that were planted there (*álamo* means "poplar"), was a cool sanctuary early in the morning, before it became crowded with families, joggers, and tourists. Throughout the park were fountains, sadly waterless when we visited, with statues depicting figures from ancient Greek and Roman mythology.[14] We spotted Mercury, Venus, Neptune, a female figure with a pitcher whose identity we were not too sure about (but later research identified as Proserpina, whose arrival heralds springtime), and two female figures positioned as if they were pouring water into a large receptacle that had holes in it. If the fountain had been working, the water would have spurted out of the holes and into the pool below it. There were no plaques with the names of the figures on them; identification was left up to the passersby.

A man sweeping the ground by the fountain with the statue of the two women pouring water saw us looking at it, nodded in its direction, and said, "*Las Aguadores.*" My Spanish is too rudimentary to strike up much of a conversation, so I made a note of the word, thanked him, and we moved on. I knew that the statue represented two of the Danaïds, who, in Greek and Roman myth, were the fifty daughters of Danaus, prince of Egypt. Danaus had a twin brother, Aegyptus, who had fifty sons. The two brothers fought incessantly over the throne of Egypt, and eventually Aegyptus threatened Danaus and insisted that he marry his daughters to Aegyptus's sons. Angry and afraid, Danaus fled with his daughters to Greece, pur-

Eternal punishment for killing their husbands. (*The Danaïds* in Alameda Park, Mexico City.)

sued by the fifty sons. Once there, Danaus seemed to change his mind. However, in secret, he gave each of his daughters a knife and ordered them, on their collective wedding night, to kill their husbands. Forty-nine of the daughters obeyed their father, but one, Hypermestra, either because she fell in love with her husband, Lynceus, or because he respected her wish not to have sex with him (versions of the tale differ[15]), spared him and helped him escape.

This is a story about patriarchal control. Women in the ancient world were supposed to obey their fathers. Once they were married, they were supposed to obey their husbands. In the afterlife, the forty-nine sisters were punished for murdering their husbands, even though they had been married for less than a day and against their will. Their punishment was to pour, in perpetuity, water into a bowl with holes in it. Like Sisyphus, doomed to push a heavy rock up a hill forever, knowing that it will always slide down before he reaches the top, the Danaïds are a striking image of punishment without end. They remind us of the impossibility of forgiveness for those who break patriarchy's rules, even when those rules seem contradictory and unfair.

The fountain with the Danaïds in the Alameda Park comes with a warning: look at what happens to women who disobey their husbands. There's something powerful, then, about the fading of their mythological meaning and the fact that the general public, like the man we met sweeping the park, now knows them simply as *Las Aguadoras*, The Water Carriers. The misogyny of the original representation of the two women is rendered impotent by the change in cultural memory. Faded meaning can be a form of resistance. I thought back to *La Diana*, whose artist had decided to name her *The Archer* but whose public had given a different name. In the case of *La Diana*, the meaning of the statue had changed from a more generic identification to a specific one from Roman mythology. With *Las Aguadoras*, the shift had worked in the other direction, from a specific mythological identification (only now used in guidebooks) to a more generic one. The process of renaming, which involves not just a change in name but also the ushering in, or the suppressing, of a mythological narrative and the gender politics of that narrative, is hard to track. There is no obvious source or instigator. It comes about through everyday talk, through the media and social media. It is probably not intentional. The other examples of protest that I've been discussing in this book have been deliberate, focused, and planned by individuals. But not all forms of protest are. Collective memory changes, and those changes can be a form of cultural resistance.

Diana, or, as the Greeks called her, Artemis, has come back in vogue in New Age feminism and in popular culture. These Dianas range from sanitized versions of the goddess to more powerful avatars.

Jean Shinoda Bolen, Jungian psychiatrist and author of the classic *Goddesses in Everywoman* (first issued in 1985) published *Artemis: The Indomitable Spirit in Everywoman* (2014), in which she argues that Artemis is the archetype of the courageous girl and woman, the one who perseveres and survives. As Gloria Steinem puffs on the back of the book: "Artemis is the archetype or goddess who can inspire us to be activists in the world." Shinoda Bolen compares the traits of the goddess to the stories and lives of strong women, real and fictional. What we get is Diana diluted, a goddess who stands for any woman who might be described as ballsy and courageous: Cheryl Strayed, Diana Nyad, Sheryl Sandberg, Elisabeth Smart, Malala Yousafzai, Eve Ensler. Katniss Everdeen, heroine of *The Hunger Games* trilogy, apparently embodies the same Artemisian independence and courage as Lisbeth Salander from Stieg Larsson's *The Girl with the Dragon Tattoo* series and Anastasia Steele from E. L. James's *Fifty Shades of Grey* books. *Holy crap!* as Lisbeth Salander would never say.

Another novel, written by Martha Beck, life coach and writer for *O Magazine*, was published in 2016. *Diana, Herself: An Allegory of Awakening* is a novel about a struggling single mother called Diana Archer (allegories are not subtle), who discovers herself when she journeys into the wilderness and learns how to use a bow and arrow and also how to listen to her intuition and to the world. Beck has a knack for capturing the serious through the absurd (the guru figure in the novel is a talking wild boar), and *Diana, Herself* is a parable of enlightenment that makes use of the motifs and qualities of the goddess Diana. At the heart of the magical tale, however, is a kernel of more subversive wisdom. Liberation only comes— for herself and for the earth—when Diana destroys patriarchy (I won't say how, but if you've never warmed to TV star survivalists, then this is the book for you).

In her book *Hunting Girls: Sexual Violence from* The Hunger Games *to Campus Rape* (2016), Kelly Oliver discusses a new trend in popular culture to represent girls as hunters, for example Katniss Everdeen, Bella Swan (*Twilight*), Tris Prior (*Divergent*), and Hanna (*Hanna*). She argues this trend is a response to an increase in violence toward girls and women: "New myths of Artemis figures defending their own virtue from the violence all around them can be interpreted as compensatory fantasies for girls and women subjected to violence, especially sexual violence, in their everyday lives."[16]

These new Artemis figures stop short, however, of doing what the real-life kick-ass heroine Diana, the Hunter of Bus Drivers does: enact revenge. Corporatized feminism does not have much time for revenge. Revenge has greater visibility as a lifestyle product than it does as an issue in feminist theory. You can paint your nails with Sweet Revenge polish by NCLA, seek retribution against your own face with Wrinkle Revenge (an "ultimate hyaluronic serum"), slap on some Yves Saint Laurent Revenge lipstick, and then work on your Revenge Body with Khloé Kardashian. All of which might be sufficient distraction to prevent you from asking tough ethical questions about whether revenge is acceptable or even necessary in circumstances when men rape women with impunity, and there are no Benson and Stabler to stop them.

Contemporary feminist writing is interested in anger but less so in revenge.[17] For that, we have to go back to the work of Andrea Dworkin. She explores the morality of revenge in her novel *Mercy*. It is a harrowing account of a woman's experiences of sexual abuse and rape, much of which resonates with Dworkin's own life story, told in her memoir *Heartbreak*; the protagonist in *Mercy* is called Andrea. Fictional Andrea becomes an avenging angel, "with a debt to settle."[18] (*Mercy* is out of print, as many of Dworkin's works are; it's one sure way of silencing her. I bought my copy from a secondhand bookshop in Berkeley. On the title page there is a handwritten dedication by the author: "For Bruce, with hope, Andrea Dworkin." *With hope.*)

Dworkin has a bad rap, even (or especially) from other feminists, and her work is often dismissed or distorted.[19] But *Mercy* is important because it raises the questions of what the difference is between revenge killing and what is now called criminalized survival, "survival" because the killing is the only way the woman can see to survive in abusive and dangerous circumstances and "criminalized" because the law is unlikely to protect her even when she kills in self-defense.

The law did not protect Cyntoia Brown. She was given a life sentence for killing a forty-three-year-old man, Johnny Allen, who had paid $150 to rape her when she was being prostituted in Nashville, Tennessee, at the age of sixteen. During the encounter, fearing for her life, she shot and killed him. Her case was reassessed in 2018, and she was released from jail, but other women are still incarcerated, even though they killed abusive men in self-defense.[20] *Mercy* also asks whether, in contexts where women are fair game, it is reasonable (or perhaps necessary) for them to kill men preemptively, whether or not they know for certain that the specific men they target have themselves hurt women. The questions that *Mercy* raises about revenge and survival are the same questions raised by the actions of Diana, the Hunter of Bus Drivers.

They are questions that take us back to the myth of Philomela and Procne. The sisters' revenge on Tereus, in killing his son and serving him up as food, made them as monstrous as their abuser was. The vigilante who shot and killed two bus drivers in Juárez in 2013 wrote her crimes into myth and, like a superhero, brought one of Mexico's national symbols, the goddess Diana, to life. But it is part of patriarchy's rigged game that the only recourse for women, in situations where they are powerless, is violence.

The women of Juárez, and women across the world, do not want to have to take revenge, any more than Procne and Philomela did. What they want is to be able to rely on the modern gods—the police, the courts, and the media—for justice.

SEVEN

ΒΣYΘNCΣ, GODDESS

I can't believe we made it.
—THE CARTERS, APESHIT

*Key to the work of changing
the world is changing the story.*
—REBECCA SOLNIT, *Call Them
by Their True Names*

APHRODITE, THE ANCIENT GREEK GODDESS OF LOVE, WAS born from the sea. More precisely, she was born from the castrated genitals of the primordial sky god Uranus, whose youngest son, Cronus, in an audacious and successful power grab, attacked his father, sliced off his genitals, and threw them into the sea off the coast of Cyprus. The severed parts floated for some time. White foam collected around them, and eventually, from the foam (the Greek word for which is *aphros*) emerged the goddess Aphrodite, "an awesome, beautiful divinity."[1]

Visual representations of Aphrodite, and her Roman counterpart Venus, tend to leave out the bit about the spumy testicles and focus instead on the emerging-gorgeously-from-the-sea part. Take *The Birth of Venus* painted by the Italian artist Sandro Botticelli in the mid-1480s. The goddess stands naked in a giant scallop shell, flanked by the wind god Zephyr and female attendants, who are most likely nymphs or person-ifications of the seasons. Flowers float down from the sky. The intimate link in the classical myth between the erotic and the violent is absent in Botticelli's painting, which offers softer and gentler pleasures.[2]

Aphrodite-Venus was, and still is, an icon of female allure. Statues of her in different poses have become an essential part of our aesthetic vocabulary. The first statue of a naked Aphrodite created a scandal when it was first displayed some-time in the fourth century BCE. The story goes that Praxite-les, an artist notorious for pushing boundaries, fashioned two statues of the goddess, one of her naked and one of her clothed. He offered the city of Cos their choice of statue, and when they chose the clothed Aphrodite, he gave the naked goddess to the city of Cnidus, where it was placed in the city's temple. The Cnidian Aphrodite became an instant tourist attraction and generated titillating tales, including one in which a young man became so attracted to the statue that he stayed in the temple after it was shut for the night and attempted to have sex with it, leaving a permanent stain on the marble.[3] Botticelli's Venus, with her hands covering (and therefore drawing attention to) her nakedness, mimics the pose of the Aphrodite of Cnidos. Venus Callipyge, Venus of the Gorgeous Buttocks, looks over her shoulder while exposing her rear, as if she is taking a "belfie." And the famously fragmented Venus de Milo, perhaps the most imitated and adapted of all images of a figure from classical myth, has become a byword for female beauty.[4]

But the relationships between Venus and women's beauty have different histories for white women and for black women. I opened this book by reminding us that *we* own culture, but that "we" hasn't always been as expansive as it should be. Classical mythology has been used to further inscribe racism in our culture and also, in the hands of creative black artists, to challenge and subvert it.

Hollywood legends such as Rita Hayworth and Joan Crawford and pop stars such as Madonna, Kylie Minogue, and Lady Gaga have represented themselves as Venus, using the iconography of the ancient goddess. Venus is shorthand for being beautiful, being put on a pedestal, and taking one's place within a distinguished lineage of stars—so much so that being photographed in front of the Venus de Milo or dressing as the goddess has become something of a celebrity cliché. This has been true for black stars too, although to a lesser extent: Lena Horne was known as "the bronze Venus" (and starred in a movie of that name), and Josephine Baker was called "the ebony Venus" and "the black Venus." (The qualifiers *bronze, ebony*, and *black* suggest that without them we are meant to assume that Venus is white.) But for black women, the legacy of Sarah Baartman (also called Sartjee

Baartman), who was given the epithet "the Hottentot Venus," casts a long shadow.

Baartman was likely a slave or an indentured servant in Cape Town, South Africa. One of the Khoikhoi people (formerly known as Hottentots), Baartman was taken to England by a Dutch trader in 1810, where she was put on public display in London as an exotic curiosity, under the name Venus Hottentot. According to a spectator at one of these shows, Baartman was "exhibited on a stage two feet high, along which she was led by her keeper, and exhibited like a wild beast; being obliged to walk, stand, or sit as he ordered her."[5] An etching published in 1811 shows Sarah Baartman semi-naked and with a Cupid riding on her protruding behind, with the words *Love and Beauty—Sartjee the Hottentot Venus*. When the display of Baartman caused consternation among abolitionists (the slave trade in England having been banned since 1807), her owner took her to France, where he continued to exhibit her until her death in 1815. Even after death, Sarah Baartman was degraded and displayed to the public. Her body was dissected to prove that she was low on the scale of civilization. Her labia were preserved in a jar of formaldehyde and were on show to the public along with her skeleton and a plaster cast of her, in profile to emphasize her buttocks, at the Musée de l'Homme in Paris until 1974. As writer Sherronda J. Brown puts it: "The story of Sarah Baartman is foundational to the simultaneous disdain for and fascination with Black women's bodies."[6]

Twenty-one years before Sarah Baartman's young death, a fictional black Venus appeared in an engraving in a book.

This depiction features a black woman in a similar pose to that of Botticelli's Venus. She is standing in a shell that is propelled across the ocean by dolphins and is accompanied by the sea god Neptune, depicted as a white man, who is carrying not his usual trident but a British flag. The engraving, called *The Voyage of the Sable Venus, from Angola to the West Indies*, was made by William Grainger to illustrate the poem "The Sable Venus. An Ode" (1793) by Isaac Teale.[7] The poem is, as a modern editor points out, "a nasty piece of work."[8] Superficially, it sets out to praise "the sable Venus" by comparing her, flatteringly, to the European Venus; the sable Venus is superior, except in the dark when the two Venuses are, we are told, equally pleasing. But the black Venus and, by extension, black women turn out to incite base lusts rather than noble desires. She is praised (that is to say, denigrated) for being more sexually available than her European counterpart, and she seduces Neptune, an inversion of the typical power relations in mythology, where the god rapes the mortal woman, and in real life, where the man rapes the enslaved woman, an inversion that both obscures and provides perverse justification for slavery. Toward the end of the poem, the focus changes from the goddess to real women, presumably slaves, in whose beauty the poet sees signs of the goddess and whom, he says, he will pursue.[9] The poem and image are slave trade propaganda and reinforce, in a coy, knowing, and sophisticated way, white supremacy.

When racism is underpinned by a cultural structure as long-standing as ancient mythology, it can be even tougher to dismantle. Many white people still have a strong emotional investment in mythological characters being portrayed as white and not black. There was an outcry in 2018 when the BBC cast black actors to play the roles of the god Zeus and warriors Achilles, Patroclus, and Aeneas in the television adaptation of Homer's *Iliad*, called *Troy, Fall of a City*.[10] This is as ridiculous and racist as the fuss made a year later when a Disney-owned company announced the casting of a black actor, Halle Bailey, as Ariel in a live-action film of *The Little Mermaid*. But it shows how proprietorial some white people can be about mythical characters. There is a desire to see themselves reflected in them.

I t takes a cultural phenomenon to rewrite a cultural script. Which brings us to Beyoncé Knowles-Carter, perhaps the most important, creative, and influential popular musician of the twenty-first century.

When Beyoncé cast herself as Venus in a series of photographs published on her Instagram page to announce her pregnancy in 2017, it was a cultural intervention that put black womanhood at the center of the Greek and Roman iconography of beauty.[11] She defied the Western artistic tradition and gave us a powerful corrective to the legacy of black Venuses that has been used to denigrate black women.

In one of the photographs, she is lying on a couch, surrounded by flowers, with her right hand behind her head and the left over her belly, mimicking the pose of the *Sleeping Venus*, a painting attributed to the Italian Renaissance painter Giorgione. In another she poses as Botticelli's *Birth of Venus*, with flowing hair and flowers falling (although these flowers are painted on her legs). Instead of in Botticelli's seashell, Beyoncé stands in lush green plants, and instead of the wind god, Nefertiti, the ancient Egyptian queen, attends her. In others she floats underwater, ethereal and otherworldly, bathed in light and swathed in cloths of yellow and other colors.[12]

The imagery in the underwater photographs casts Beyoncé as Osun (also known as Oshun), a Yoruba *orisha* (spirit) of fresh water, who is connected with fertility, beauty, and love and who gives her name to the Osun River in Nigeria, and as Yemoja, the Yoruban goddess of the ocean, who is the mother of all the *orishas* and a protector of pregnant women.

Part of the brilliance of Beyoncé's photographs is that she plays Venus as a mother. The ancient goddess did in fact have children, notably the hero Aeneas who was said to have founded the city of Rome, and she was worshipped as Venus Genetrix (Venus in her aspect as a mother), but little modern art focuses upon the goddess in this role, nor have other pop stars been obviously pregnant when they played the goddess. Being pregnant and including her first child, Blue Ivy, in some of the photographs allows Beyoncé to escape the common trap for black Venuses: denigration and hypersexualization.

Beyoncé changes the story about which mythological figures are valued and which cultural and mythological reference points matter when she makes Venus share her throne with

Beyoncé is many goddesses: here as Osun and Venus, as well as Mary, mother of Jesus. (In a performance at the 2017 Grammy Awards.)

African deities. She did something similar when she dressed as the ancient Egyptian queen Nefertiti, as part of her stage performance at Coachella in 2018, and as Queen Amanishakheto, an ancient Nubian warrior from Meroe in what is now Sudan, at the Wearable Art Gala in 2018. During her extraordinary performance at the Grammy Awards ceremony in 2017, Beyoncé's persona changed from goddess to goddess, icon to icon. She was Osun, swathed in yellow scarves, and Venus, garlanded in flowers, and Mary, mother of Jesus.

In 1979 the African American feminist poet and civil rights activist Audre Lorde wrote a letter to the white American feminist theologian Mary Daly, taking Daly to task for writing a book (*Gyn/Ecology: The Metaethics of Radical Feminism*, 1978) about goddesses and female power that only featured Western European goddesses and women, except when considering Africans as victims (in a discussion of genital mutilation).[13] "So I wondered, why doesn't Mary deal with Afrekete as an example?" she wrote. "Why are her goddess images only white, western European, judea-christian? Where was Afrekete, Yemanje, Oyo, and Mawulisa? . . . I began to feel my history and my mythic background distorted by the absence of any images of my foremothers in power."

It is as if Beyoncé, a generation later, is having the same argument with, and through, popular culture, as Lorde had with Daly. It is an argument that goes to the heart of continuing culture wars about classical mythology and, more broadly, classical antiquity, in the academy and on the streets.

It is an important part of European and American national identities and to the construction of "the West" that they are the heirs to (an idealized version of) ancient Greece and Rome. An extreme version of this invented tradition is seen in the way that fascist groups raid classical antiquity, as the Nazi Party did in the 1940s, to create a tradition of European and white supremacy. The American Identity Movement (formerly Identity Europa) is a white nationalist organization that was involved in planning the 2017 Unite the Right rally in Charlottesville, Virginia, in which activist Heather Heyer was killed. Their aim is to build "European identity and solidarity" through stressing what they claim is America's European, non-Semitic heritage. The posters that they have put up to recruit students on university and college campuses have the group's name printed over photographs of the heads of Greek and Roman statues, making an implicit association between white marble and white supremacy and between American identity and ancient Greece and Rome.[14]

Online "red pill" communities—an assortment of angry and anonymous men who see themselves as victimized by women and people of color—appropriate authors and ideas from classical antiquity to give their misogynist and racist ideas intellectual validation, as Donna Zuckerberg has shown in her book *Not All White Men*.[15] Less extreme, but perhaps more pernicious, is the idea that classical antiquity, especially Athens, was exceptionally advanced and cultured and was the foundation for Western civilization (a phrase that is rapidly becoming code for white, Euro-American superiority, whether we intend it to signify that or not).[16]

The National Geographic series *The Greeks: Crucible of Civilization*, which first aired on PBS in 2016, promotes this idea of the "Greek miracle": "They were an extraordinary people born of white rock and blue sea. Quite simply, the Greeks created our world. Uncover the origin story of Western civilization, as the early Greeks rise from nothing and change everything." "The story of the Greeks," we are told in magisterial tones over a swelling orchestra, "is the story of us." The notion that the Greeks rose "from nothing" cannot be true. We know that they had considerable cultural contact with ancient Egyptians and Phoenicians (who developed the very first alphabet). It's a notion that has its origins in ancient Athenian myths that represented the Athenians as auto-chthonous, as having sprung up from the Athenian land itself, from nothing, in contrast to nomadic foreign tribes that came from all over.[17]

It is important to recognize that the ancient Greeks and Romans have given us a rich and influential inheritance of mythology, philosophy, architecture, theater, and politics. We do not need to hide the destructive aspects of these leg-acies, nor do we need to use antiquity to perpetrate myths of European and Western superiority to appreciate the value of ancient Greece and Rome.

In sum, as artist Kara Walker puts it, archly, in a creative essay that excoriates the racism of Austrian history, white Europeans "often resort to themes of Classical Antiquity to describe the enormity of [their] Selves to the Rest of Human-ity."[18] It is within this context that Beyoncé, through her care-fully curated persona, says "Boy Bye" to all that and insists instead on centering African history and myth and changing the valence and value of Greek and Roman myth. In making visible her "foremothers in power," she makes visible black women's pasts and energizes their futures.

Some of our most memorable encounters with Greek and Roman myths happen in museums, where ancient statues, pediments, and vase paintings jostle with later European paint-ings to tell their stories. But museums are not uncomplicated

spaces of display: facing repeated accusations of theft, uneth-
ical acquisition and display of objects, and cultural appropriation, museums are at the forefront of the question of who
owns culture. (Sarah Baartman's remains were only returned
by the Museé de l'Homme to South Africa for interment in
2002.) Museums do not just display culture; they create it. Cu-
rators are in privileged positions to decide what to include and
what to exclude and which artists and whose myths count.

The big picture is miserable. The Louvre Museum in
Paris, for example, houses roughly six thousand paintings, but
only twenty-one women artists have works in the collection,
and none are identified as women of color.[19] There are few
paintings and statues that feature people of color who are not
slaves. Most of the art from Africa, Asia, Oceania, and the
Americas is housed in a separate museum (the Museé du Quai
Branly); only a small collection is displayed in the Pavillon
des Sessions of the Denon wing in the Louvre. Once a royal
palace, with a private art collection, the Louvre was turned
into a national and free space in 1783. Its layout was designed
to indicate that France was the rightful heir to the traditions
of ancient Egypt, Greece, Rome, and the Italian Renaissance;
the visitor went through these galleries with the tour culmi-
nating in French academic painting. Many of its masterpieces
were war booty, plundered by Napoleon Bonaparte. Crowned
emperor of France in 1804, Napoleon brought back objects
from his military campaigns, proclaiming France and its colonial victories, the New Rome.

It must be about time, then, to go APESHIT.

APESHIT is what happened when Beyoncé and Jay-Z took over the Louvre.

It was the first music video to be released from the Carters' album *Everything Is Love*.[20] Filmed inside the museum in May 2018, it is an exhilarating six minutes whose stunning images and sharp juxtapositions of ancient and modern reflect upon race, art, and resistance. The video criticizes the exclusion of black people and culture from the Louvre, but it also goes beyond that, by reimagining the space and its collections in ways that create new icons, perspectives, and priorities. It acts as a kind of restorative mythmaking.

The song has two refrains: "I can't believe we made it" and "Have you ever seen a crowd going apeshit?" They take on different shades of meaning at different moments in the video. Some of them underscore the themes of cultural ownership and of protest.

Protest involves the taking up of space. Black people in the United States cannot inhabit public spaces without the risk that white people will call the police to report them for entirely innocuous activities: for eating lunch quietly on their college campus, hanging out in Starbucks, swimming in their community pool with their family, sheltering in the rain in a doorway while waiting for a ride, barbecuing in the park, or being an eight-year-old selling water on the sidewalk in front of their home. Enjoying public space is, for black people, a dangerous business.

It is the inhospitable space of the Louvre that Beyoncé, Jay-Z, and their dancers, all men and women of color, take over ("I can't believe we've made it"). It is in this space that they sing and rap and dance, with a few moments of quiet, except for a bell in the distance and muffled traffic noise, capturing the typical hush of a museum, before the music starts. It is in this space that Beyoncé dances in formation with her dancers, wearing nude bodysuits of different skin colors, in front of Jacques-Louis David's *The Consecration of the Emperor Napoleon and the Coronation of the Empress Joséphine*, with her place in the choreography strategically positioned so that Napoleon crowns her instead of Joséphine; one Creole woman replaces another, and Beyoncé and Jay-Z become the new royalty of the Louvre.[21] It is in this space that the dancers replace statues and gyrate on pedestals, their dynamic energy juxtaposed with the immobility of the marble figures. There is sheer joy in the contrasts here: between the white bodies on the walls and the black bodies in front of them, between the powerful movement of the dancers and the stillness of the artwork, between the reverent silence of the museum and the exuberant sound of the music.

Toward the beginning of the video we see Beyoncé and Jay-Z in exquisite pink and turquoise suits standing in front of the *Mona Lisa*. Here, and throughout the video, the human figures in the foreground are mesmerizing, compelling the viewer's eye in ways that make the paintings in their frames merely backdrops to the real art.[22] When Beyoncé dances maniacally in front of the Nike of Samothrace, the massive winged statue that personifies Victory (Nike means "victory"; hence the name of the famous brand of sneakers), agitating her robe's swathes of white and gray material, she is Nike come to life. It is Beyoncé and Jay-Z who become the works of art, the mythic figures, the Brand New Ancients.[23]

When Beyoncé dances as the Nike of Samothrace and when she stands in front of the Venus de Milo, with her body mimicking the S-shaped pose of the statue but contrasting with its amputated helplessness, the juxtaposition of her black body with the white marble challenges long-held assumptions about whiteness, antiquity, and beauty. Greek and Roman white marble statues have become idealized and romanticized since the sixteenth century and in the popular imagination, and their whiteness has become conflated with white skin color. White marble "skin" has, in turn, become equated with beauty. In fact, marble statues were originally brightly painted in bold colors that included red, green, yellow, brown, white, black, and gold; they were polychromous. Through the ravages of time, most of the color has been rubbed off, but modern technological advances are able to detect vestiges of the paint, and we are able to reconstruct what some of the statues looked like when they were first viewed. I confess that when I first saw one of these reconstructions, I found it shocking. So deeply held was my belief in the beauty of white marble that the polychromy of ancient statues seemed lurid and, if I'm honest, a bit tacky.

The polychromy of ancient statues has upset people politically, as well as aesthetically. When ancient historian Sarah

Bond wrote about how statues were not all white, both in the sense that they were not unpainted and in the sense that they did not only portray white people (a category that the Greeks and Romans would not have understood—they divided people up by their ethnic denominations: Celts, Ethiopians, Greeks, and so on, not by race in our terms), she faced outrage and abuse. Classicist Mary Beard got a similar response when she affirmed that ancient Rome was a multicultural and (in our terms) multiracial society. "Whiteness is a metaphor for power," said James Baldwin, and many do not want to give up that power or to give up the whiteness of ancient statues. Beyoncé's embodiment of the Nike of Samothrace and the Venus de Milo is a visual intervention in this controversy and a gorgeous and artistic dismissal of the old lies that conflate whiteness of marble with ideal beauty.

When Jay-Z and Beyoncé flank, and then rap in front of, the Great Sphinx of Tanis, the monumental Egyptian figure with the body of a lion and the head of a king, thought to date to the Old Kingdom (around 2600 BCE), the images have political as well as artistic resonances. The Louvre displays Egyptian antiquities along with the Greek and Roman collections as part of the "European" art. In doing so, it claims Egyptian art as part of the heritage of French culture and excludes it from the African art collections. The refrain of the song takes on a specific meaning when Beyoncé and Jay-Z sing it in front of the Sphinx: "I can't believe we made it" becomes specific and possessive, staking a claim to the Sphinx as a monument created by, and belonging to, Africans and their descendants.[24]

A PESHIT repeatedly alters our perspectives on race through its reframing of art: swapping background for foreground (as when the *Mona Lisa* and *The Coronation of the Empress Joséphine* become the backdrop to the Carters and the dancers in front of them) and through focusing on details of paintings and making the details fill the screen as artworks in their own right. This technique is most striking when used to spotlight the faces of black servants in Veronese's *The Wedding Feast at Cana*. From a painting so densely packed with people at a banquet that it is hard to spot the few black figures even when you are searching for them, APESHIT creates new art that gives the overlooked—people of color—the starring roles.

The most explicit reference to protest comes in the latter half of the video, with a lingering shot of young black men taking the knee outside the Louvre, alluding to the National Football League player protests against police killings of unarmed black men, which comes directly after a shot of a classical statue in a similar pose. The statue, a Roman version of a Greek work by the artist Lysippus (who is said also to have been commissioned by Alexander the Great to paint his portrait), is thought to represent the god Hermes adjusting his shoe while listening to orders from his father Zeus, king of the Olympian gods; it is known as Hermes Tying His Sandal.[25] Over the image of the statue, Jay-Z sings lyrics that are critical of the NFL, the organization that Colin Kaepernick has accused of colluding to keep him off the field because of his protests during the national anthem before games. Once one of the game's most brilliant quarterbacks, Kaepernick has not been given work since he started protesting in 2016. The juxtaposition of the image of Hermes with his knee bent inside the Louvre with that of the kneeling protestors outside the Louvre co-opts the statue, bringing the ancient god on board as part of the modern protest. Hermes becomes an advocate for black lives mattering; he is given a better purpose than fiddling with his footwear. The modern ennobles the classical (a reversal of the expected dynamic). The idea that Hermes is listening to Zeus while he ties his sandal is a bit fanciful of art historians; he certainly looks as if he has been disturbed, but we cannot be sure by whom or what. However, that is the myth that has adhered to the statue, and it gives "taking the knee" divine imprimatur. After all (NFL, are you listening?), things don't go well in Greek myths for fools who do not obey Zeus.

It is not just the *content* of APESHIT (the lyrics and the things featured in the video) that is a form of protest, but also the *process* in which it engages the viewer and listener. The insistence that the viewer makes connections, the refusal to simplify, and the sheer richness of the historical, artistic, and ideological textures created: all of this is a form of cultural resistance.[26]

There is a long history of people actually going apeshit in the Louvre and other museums, with both impulsive and carefully planned attacks on artwork. In 1914, Mary Richardson walked into London's National Gallery and slashed with a meat cleaver Diego Velasquez's painting of a naked Venus gazing into her mirror (known as the Rokeby Venus). She was protesting the arrest of fellow suffragette Emmeline Pankhurst. She wrote a statement explaining her actions, in which she makes clear that her choice of Venus as a target was deliberate: "I have tried to destroy the picture of the most beautiful woman in mythological history as a protest against the Government for destroying Mrs Pankhurst, who is the most beautiful character in modern history. Justice is an element of beauty as much as colour and outline on canvas." She goes on to declare that the outcry about the destruction of a picture, but not about the destruction of people, is "moral and political humbug and hypocrisy."

More recently in the Louvre, in 2009, a Russian woman, said to have been frustrated when she was turned down for French citizenship, waged a more spontaneous protest when she lobbed a mug that she had just purchased in the Louvre gift shop at the *Mona Lisa*: "Screams erupted from the 40-odd tourists jostling for position around Leonardo da Vinci's enigmatic painted lady when the empty terracotta mug flew over their heads and smashed into the portrait." The bulletproof glass ensured that no damage was done.

But, unlike these scandals, the Carters' protest is as carefully curated as the museum collections and with a sharper and more politically aware eye. Rewriting cultural narratives of race and power, subverting white spaces, and insisting on the complexity of the connections that we can and should make is more effective than throwing a mug at the *Mona Lisa* or slashing a painting. APESHIT, like Beyoncé's pregnancy photographs, and public performances, brilliantly fuses ancient Greek, Roman, and Egyptian mythological figures and artwork with images from modern African American art and uses them to advocate for social justice. Antiquity (Greek, Roman, Yoruba, Egyptian) and the many layers lent to antiquity by later artists are essential parts of Beyoncé's feminist mythmaking.

"Key to the work of changing the world is changing the story," Rebecca Solnit reminds us.[27] Beyoncé is far from the only artist to change the story when it comes to classical mythology, black womanhood, and antiquity.[28] Kara Walker's installation A *Subtlety, or the Marvelous Sugar Baby* (2014), a massive sugar sphinx-mammy displayed in an old sugar factory in Brooklyn, and her temporary exhibition *Safety Curtain at the Vienna State Opera House* (1998–1999) both play, disconcertingly and provocatively, with the clash between figures from ancient myth and figures from black history and culture (the Egyptian and Greek sphinxes, the caricature of the mammy, the myth of Orpheus and Eurydice, and the minstrel show character Mr. Tambo, the always cheerful musician).[29] Hip-hop artist Monae Smith (aka Medusa, "the lyrical seducer") and performance artist and poet Dorothea Smartt (in her collection of poems *Connecting Medium*, 2001) reconfigure Medusa through their own experiences as queer black women and, in very different ways, change Medusa's story to one of black women's empowerment and resilience in the face of white oppression.[30] And Robin Coste Lewis's poetry collection *Voyage of the Sable Venus* (2015) contains a poem, exhaustively researched, that is composed entirely of the "titles, catalog entries, or exhibit descriptions" of objects in museums that depict the black female form. She both exposes the ugliness of museum curating and, in a moving epilogue to her collection, restores the humanity of the "Sable Venus."[31] Beyoncé is both part of a wave of revisionist and reparative black women's mythmaking, as well as her own singular goddess.

I doubt that we have heard the last of her subversive re-creation of antiquity. As I write this, newspapers are reporting that the Carters are trying to film a video in the Colosseum in Rome, the amphitheater built by emperors of the Flavian dynasty, which was used for gladiatorial contests, some of which reenacted ancient mythological scenes. Apparently, the Carters' request has been rejected. But my money's on Beyoncé and Jay-Z. I can't believe they won't make it.

EIGHT

TRANSMYTHOLOGY

I never had to do anything, I said. I'm lucky. I
was born mythless. I grew up mythless.

No you didn't. Nobody grows up mythless,
Robin said. It's what we do with the myths we
grow up with that matters.
—ALI SMITH, *Girl Meets Boy*

A POPULAR STORY IN ANCIENT GREECE AND ROME TELLS OF
the sex change of a resourceful young woman, named Caenis,
to a young man, named Caeneus:

> Caeneus, they say, used to be a woman. Neptune desired
> her, but she said that there was no way she would sleep with
> him unless he swore to make her whatever she wanted.
> When Neptune had sworn agreement, she said that he
> should "make me a man." Bound by his oath, Neptune did
> this, and he did not get the pleasure of sex.[1]

In other, more elaborate, versions of the tale, Caenis became not just an ordinary man but one who was invulnerable, who could not in any way, be penetrated. (There is a lot of phallic imagery in this myth, as if to emphasize Caeneus's newly male body.) Caeneus was a superhero, a warrior who worshipped his spear and led his tribe, the Lapiths, into war. Eventually, he was overcome by the centaurs, creatures whose lower bodies were equine and upper bodies, human, who bashed him into the earth with the trunks of pine trees. The myth has different endings: some relate that Caeneus was driven underground, others that he changed once again, this time into a bird with golden wings.

Caenis is one of several figures in classical myths that change their sex, whose gender does not fit the sex they are assigned at birth, or whose gender is fluid. Their stories provide inspiration and affirmation for transgender and gender-queer people today. We look to antiquity to provide examples of human behavior, ways of living that confirm, challenge, and expand the possibilities for how we live today. We don't exist in a temporal vacuum. We turn to the past for positive ways of thinking about the present and the future.

This is borne out by the responses of trans and gender-queer youth to a summer 2018 survey called "The Impact of Classics on Queer Youth Identity Formation." It was created and distributed, via social media, by Hannah Clarke, an undergraduate at Miami University in Ohio, majoring in classical humanities, creative writing, and women's, gender, and sexuality studies.[2] One and a half thousand people responded, from teenagers to those in their midtwenties. The respondents identified themselves as genderqueer, lesbian, gay, nonbinary, pansexual, asexual, trans man, trans woman, questioning, genderfluid, fluidflux, and demigirl, and various combinations thereof. Such jeweled words, so many possibilities. When I was young, women were straight, bisexual, or lesbian. (For the record, I am a cis woman and bisexual, which is a pity because bisexual is society's least favored orientation, tolerated but a bit of a disappointment. It is the digestive biscuit in the cookie selection box of sexual definitions.) The survey asked about how LGBTQ+ mythological figures and stories matter to young people, in the classroom and in popular media.

Here are just a few of the responses:

"I think it would have helped me to be more comfortable in myself to have learned earlier on that queer narratives have existed for millennia, and that stories I loved featured people like me."

"It [the myth of Iphis and Ianthe] matters to me because it shows that life according to gender and sexuality in the binary isn't something that has been held as true and concrete for all of history."

"Learning about LGBTQ figures in the classroom helped me feel validated."

"It makes queerness visible in a way that makes me feel seen."

The responses show that young queer people are drawn to figures from ancient myth who challenge the idea that what is "normal" and "natural" are unchanging and fixed categories. Also, that they have a deep need to feel affirmed, validated, less lonely, and more visible, and that ancient myths with queer story lines help to meet this need. Most mentioned were Sappho, Dionysus, Teiresias, and Achilles and Patroclus, but also Loki, an androgynous Norse god (played in the Thor movies by the actor Tom Hiddleston, who, as it happens, took my course "Sexual Ethics in Ancient Greece and Rome" as part of his undergraduate Classics degree at Cambridge University; he can tell you about the history of androgyny as well as act the part), and the myths of Iphis and Ianthe, Salmacis and Hermaphroditus, and Caeneus.

The role of Greek myth as queer idealism has a long history. Psychoanalysis and sexology emerged in the nineteenth century and were influenced by ancient myths and ideas about desire.[3] These disciplines pathologized homosexuality and lesbianism and, in categorizing them as psychologically abnormal and unhealthy, gave scientific authority to the criminalization of gay and lesbian relationships. The same period saw a surge in advocacy for "Greek love," notably, in England, through the writers John Addington Symonds and Oscar Wilde.[4] "I know Hyacinthus whom Apollo loved so madly, was you in Greek days" wrote Oscar Wilde to his beloved Alfred, Lord Douglas, two years before the playwright's trial for "gross indecency" in London in 1895.

In ancient Greece, love affairs between men were the norm. Elite men (we have less evidence about poorer men and slaves) were expected to marry women and have love affairs with men (as well as sex with prostitutes and slaves of both sexes). Romantic relationships between men were largely celebrated, as long as they were between an older man and a younger boy. Quite how large an age gap was involved is a matter for debate among scholars. They are likely to have included relationships between a youth aged eighteen and a man aged twenty, but also between boys younger than that and men who were older.[5]

So, love between men in ancient Greece overlaps in part with what we would call homosexuality and in part with what we would call child abuse, depending on the ages of the people involved at the time and the age of consent laws where we live now. This is also true of relationships between men and women or girls; childhood ended much earlier in those times. But the way that the Greeks thought about sexual relationships was a bit different from the way we do today. The ancient Greeks and Romans thought in terms of sexual practices, rather than sexual orientations or identities. They were more concerned with whether a man was self-controlled in his expressions of desire than with the sex of the person he desired. Even though I am going to use modern terms when discussing the ancient world, they are strictly speaking anachronistic. It would not have made sense to ask a man in fifth-century Athens if he was gay or straight.

Myths reflected reality. Gods and humans in Greek mythology took male lovers. Zeus abducted the Trojan youth
Ganymede (this was hardly consensual; no human could reject Zeus). Achilles, the brilliant warrior whose tale is told in
Homer's *Iliad*, was the lover of Patroclus and was heartbroken
when he was killed.[6] The philosopher Plato wrote his own
myths about gay love.[7]

It was very different for women, who were not supposed
to do much desiring of any kind. Here the poet Sappho is an
important exception. An acclaimed writer of exquisite poetry, she wrote about love affairs between women, as well
as between women and men. Our word *lesbian* is derived
from the Greek island of Lesbos where she lived and worked
around 620–560 BCE. We know very little about Sappho,
and she was so extraordinary that she became something of
a myth, even in antiquity. In the nineteenth century, when
the visibility of lesbian love increased, Sappho, "the original
lesbian," proved inspirational.[8] And, as the respondents to
the Queer Youth survey show, she continues to be an icon
for lesbian and bisexual women.

The foundational role that classical myth has played in
constructing gay and lesbian identities and inspiring
gays and lesbians sets an agenda: to investigate whether it can
play a similar role for trans, intersex, and gender nonbinary
identities and lives. There is little written on the importance

of ancient models for trans, intersex, and gender nonbinary people.[9] Excavating their mythic predecessors might provide cultural affirmation and be a small step further toward social acceptance and equality.

At first glance, this is not an easy task. Classical antiquity was not an accepting place for intersex folk; there are accounts of people being ostracized and even killed.[10] Several myths feature males impersonating women by dressing in women's clothes or taking a female form and entering women-only spaces. They always pose a sexual threat to women and often rape or attempt to rape women. Achilles, when he was a boy, was hidden in a girls' school, where he lived as a girl; his mother wanted to prevent him from going to fight in the Trojan War, after it was prophesied that he would die there. He ended up raping a fellow student, Deidamia. Jupiter, lusting after the hunter Callisto, gained access to her and violently raped her by visiting her in the form of the goddess Diana, her companion.[11] Myth here functions to spread fear; it cultivates a similar prejudiced alarmism as today's "bathroom panic."

The myths of Teiresias, Salmacis and Hermaphroditus, Iphys and Ianthe, and Caeneus all have aspects that jar with modern sexual politics and might even be thought to be queerphobic. When I read the responses to the Queer Youth survey, my first reaction was puzzlement. My inner philologist wanted to cry out, "You are misreading these myths!"

But if the myths are meaningful to genderqueer people, then that in itself is worth heeding. Interpreting myth is always a selective business. As Kathy Acker, quoted in the preface to

Ali Smith's novel *Girl Meets Boy*, puts it, "There is the need for narrative and the simultaneous need to escape the prison-house of the story—to misquote." As we've seen repeatedly in this book, myths are read selectively, re-created, adapted, cut and pasted, and they always have been, especially in antiquity. The different versions of myths operated collectively as a kind of conversation, later versions responding to earlier, like contributions to a long-running debate. What I found when I went back to the ancient myths and looked at them afresh is that my inner philologist was wrong. Some contain more trans-affirmative elements than I had realized; looking at myths with a "queer eye" unlocks levels that would otherwise remain hidden. In other words, it is not always necessary to misquote after all.

The most detailed account of the myth of Caeneus is found in Ovid's *Metamorphoses*.[12] In Ovid's version, Neptune raped the young woman Caenis and afterward offered to grant her whatever wish she chose. Her wish was "to cease to be a woman" so that she would never experience pain like that again. As she uttered these words, she transitioned into Caeneus:

> *She spoke her last*
> *Words in a deeper tone; they might well seem*
> *A man's voice.*

Neptune gave Caeneus an additional power, that of physical invulnerability. He could not ever again be penetrated, even by a spear or sword.

This story is troubling when seen through a modern lens; life-affirming choices need not spring from ruin. Being transgender typically involves a process of realizing that your gender does not match your sex, not, as in Caeneus's story, an immediate change from one sex to another. Some trans people decide physically to change their bodies, with hormones and through surgery, so that their physicality is more aligned with their gender, and others choose not to do so or cannot afford to do so. Trans men do not choose to become men to escape the vulnerabilities of being women; they realize that they are men. On the face of it, the Caeneus myth is a damaging misrepresentation.

And yet, Ovid is never straightforward. Nestor, a wise old man, is the narrator of the tale about Caeneus, and the way that he tells the story is important. He admits that his memory is not great and, although he insists that he remembers the tale of Caeneus very well, also distances himself from what happened with phrases that introduce uncertainty about the truth of his account, such as "as rumor had it" and "this also was part of the same rumor."[13] Other aspects of the myth also ring alarm bells for readers familiar with the tropes of ancient stories. Caenis is described as a "celebrated beauty," "loveliest of all the girls in Thessaly." We are told that she had many suitors, but "Caenis married no one." Why not? It is a very odd thing for girls of marriageable age in stories like this not to marry. Also odd is the fact that Caenis is not punished after being raped; most women in the *Metamorphoses* who are raped are punished afterward. We could read Caeneus's eventual defeat by the centaurs as a punishment, but if so, it is a punishment that is very much delayed, after a long period of happiness. Nestor also tells us that one version of the story has Caeneus escaping the centaurs by metamorphosing into a bird. Finally, after he is rewarded with the granting of his wish, Caeneus rejoices not in being free from the threat of being raped (the ostensible reason for his transitioning) but in being a man and in spending his days "doing men's activities."

None of these details fit with the narrative that Caeneus transitions to avoid rape. They hint, instead, at a different story, one in which Caeneus transitioned because he always knew that he was a man, and Neptune's wish gave him the opportunity to fully live as one. This line of interpretation is reinforced by the oldest version of the Caeneus tale that survives. It is in a fragment from the myth collector Akousilaus: "Neptune had sex with Caenis, daughter of Elatos. Then—for it was not right for him to have children with him nor anyone else—Neptune turned him into an invulnerable man, who had the greatest strength of the men at that time. Whenever anyone tried to strike him with iron or bronze, they were completely defeated."[14] The pronouns tell a story. In the Greek it is clear that Caenis is a female when Neptune has sex with her because the feminine pronoun is used in addition to the female form of the name. However, in the next sentence, both pronouns are him: "it was not right for him to have children with him nor anyone else" presumably this means that it was not right for Caenis to have children with Neptune, rather than the other way around, because Neptune frequently had children with women he raped, but the Greek is unclear. Then "Neptune turned *him* into an invulnerable man": once again, Caenis is gendered male *before* Neptune changes him.

Although rape is not a trigger for trans men to transition, impermeability to rape and physical violence is very much a fantasy of many trans men and women. Rape and physical assault are real fears for trans people, especially trans women of color, who are disproportionately targeted.[15] In Ovid, the fantasy of impermeability plays out in a later scene in which Caeneus is the target of what we would call transphobic bigotry, the kind of nastiness that often precedes a physical attack. Some time after transitioning, Caeneus, along with his comrades, finds himself in a battle with the centaurs. Caeneus faces the centaur Latreus, who hurls abuse at him:

> Do I have to deal with you too, Caenis!
> To me you will always be a woman,
> To me you will always be Caenis! Doesn't your birth
> Remind you, don't you remember for what act you
>   were given the reward of a fake male appearance?
>   Just think what you were born as, or what you have
>   suffered.
> Go away! Go back to your spinning wheel
> And wool-basket! Spin the thread with your practiced
>   hand. Leave wars to men![16]

What happens next is, therefore, deeply satisfying. Caeneus responds by spearing the centaur deep into his middle. "Mad with pain," Latreus fights back, thrusting his lance into Caeneus's unprotected face. It did not break Caeneus's skin, and the description of the weapon's failure mocks his opponent: "Away it bounced, like hailstone from a roof, or a small pebble from a hollow drum." The centaur tries again and rams his sword into Caeneus's groin. The metal makes a loud thud, "as if it had struck marble," and the blade shatters. Caeneus slays Latreus and remains impervious to attack by a mob of other centaurs. How the story ends, says Nestor, "remains uncertain." The centaurs bury Caeneus under a vast mound of rocks and uprooted trees, until he struggles to breathe.

In other versions of the myth, the centaurs hammer Caeneus into the ground, an image that for me has become fused with a metaphor used by the feminist critic Sara Ahmed for transphobia within feminism, which "is experienced as a hammering, a constant chipping away at trans existence" and for a more productive joining forces of feminists and trans people so that both can chip away at patriarchy: "an affinity of hammers."[17]

Ovid's Nestor continues to narrate the story: he says that some think that the weight of the wood pushed Caeneus right down into the underworld, but Mopsus the seer (and grandson of the more famous seer Teiresias, whose myth we shall turn to in a moment) saw fly up from the middle of the mound a bird with golden wings, and Mopsus celebrates him as once a great hero and now a unique bird. This is a happy ending to a myth about an extraordinary, mythical trans man.

Centaurs bash Caeneus into the ground (here with jars). (Phoenician sarcophagus, fifth century BCE.)

In today's world, to be genderfluid is to be marginalized. Anyone relegated to ticking "other" on forms has a pretty hard time of it in our society. People like Eddie Izzard, who, as Izzard describes it in his memoir *Believe Me: A Memoir of Love, Death, and Jazz Chickens*, have "boy days" and "girl days" are not well represented in our culture.[18] But in classical antiquity, many of the gods were genderfluid. We think (patchy evidence makes this somewhat speculative) that the earliest gods in ancient Rome had no gender. Some scholars argue that Venus originally derived from the noun *venus*, which denoted an abstract quality of physical charm or grace. That noun was classified as neuter (rather than masculine or feminine), and so Venus originally had no sex.[19] One ancient writer explains a statue that he has seen in Cyprus called Aphroditus, or Venus the Nurturer, that depicts Venus with a beard and male genitalia. "When sacrificing to her," we are told, "men wear women's clothing and women men's clothing, because she is considered to be at once male and female."[20]

The Roman god Vertumnus had no fixed identity whatsoever; he changed his gender, age, and physical form at will.[21] Vertumnus was the deity of the seasons, change, and the flourishing of plants. There's a play in his name on the Latin word *vertere*, which means "to change." An ancient scholar named Servius wrote: "Divine powers are seen to be of each sex, since they are incorporeal and adopt whatever physique they wish."[22] There was considerable discussion about this in antiquity; not everyone agreed with Servius, but there are considerable positive paradigms here to build the foundations of a history of genderfluidity. As one respondent to Hannah Clarke's survey said, "If Gods are genderfluid . . . why should I feel alone in my fluidity?"

Who derives the most pleasure from sex, men or women? This question was put to the mythical prophet Teiresias, who lived as a man and as a woman. Teiresias was out walking when he saw two snakes having sex. He struck one of them with his stick and became a woman. Teiresias lived as a woman for eight years (and in one version of the myth became pregnant and gave birth to a child during this time), until one day he came across another (or perhaps the same) pair of coupling snakes. He struck one of them with his stick again and regained his male body. A while later, Zeus and Hera were arguing about who derives the most pleasure from sex—men or women—and they decided to consult Teiresias because he alone had the experience to know for sure. Teiresias answered that women got nine times more pleasure than men, a response that annoyed Hera so greatly that she gouged his eyes out. Zeus compensated him for his blindness with the gift of prophecy and a life lasting for seven generations.[23] Why was Hera so angered by Teiresias's answer? We don't know for sure. A likely theory is that it revealed women to be immoderate and lustful: a secret better kept hidden.

The myth of Teiresias does not map easily onto modern trans narratives.[24] It could be read as a tale of transition regret; after living as a woman for a long period of time, Teiresias chooses to change back to the sex that they were assigned at birth. The respondents to the Queer Youth survey, however, focused on Teiresias's superhuman powers of divination. Teiresias was one of the ancient myths that inspired the novelist Jeffrey Eugenides to write *Middlesex*, a fictional tale about the life of Cal (originally Callie, from Calliope, the name of one of the muses) Stephanides, an intersex man of Greek descent, who emigrates to the United States.[25] Cal is intersex through an unusual genetic condition; as Cal puts it at the beginning of the novel, "Sing now, O Muse, of the recessive mutation on my fifth chromosome." *Middlesex* broke new ground; it is one of the few works of literature to have an intersex character as the main protagonist.

Essential to Cal Stephanides's journey of self-discovery is the myth of Hermaphroditus, from which we get our word *hermaphrodite*, a term that is rarely used now because of its pejorative connotations. Callie goes to the New York Public Library to look up the meaning of hermaphrodite and is upset when the dictionary definition ends with "see synonyms at MONSTER."[26] In some accounts of the Hermaphroditus myth, Hermaphroditus, the son of the gods Hermes and Aphrodite, was intersex from birth. Ovid, however, tells a different story, one in which his sex was intimated at birth (his appearance showed aspects of both of his parents) but was more directly caused by an extraordinary metamorphosis. Hermaphroditus was a handsome youth whose beauty inflamed the desire of a water nymph called Salmacis. When he rejected her advances, Salmacis, whom Ovid's storyteller describes in terms typically used of male rapists, tricks Hermaphroditus into diving naked into her pool and merges with him physically so that the two of them will never again be apart:

> They are not two, but have a dual appearance, not
>   describable as woman
> Nor as boy, they appear to be neither—and both.[27]

From that time on, the story goes, men who bathe in the pool are made soft and effeminate. Salmacis's fountain can still be visited in the city of Bodrum, on the south coast of Turkey.

The Roman statue the Sleeping Hermaphroditus, on display at the Louvre, plays a joke on the viewer. Viewed from behind, the statue looks like a woman, with female hips. Walk round to the front and you see Hermaphroditus's genitals and the swell of their breasts. But what strikes me is the beauty of the sleeping figure: there is nothing monstrous about Hermaphroditus. Despite some disturbing elements in the myth (the sexual assault and the effeminizing properties of the fountain), Hermaphroditus introduces a figure who breaks our sexual categories (boy or girl?) and—this part is crucial— who is exquisitely beautiful.

The myth of Iphis and Ianthe is the only myth about lesbian desire that survives from classical antiquity. It is also a foundational myth for trans men, however uncomfortably (or impossibly) those two interpretations fit together.

The story goes that Ligdus and his wife, Telethusa, were expecting a child, but Ligdus insisted that if the baby was a girl, then Telethusa had to dispose of her. Telethusa gave birth to a girl and prayed to the goddess Isis who advised her to bring the child up as a boy, concealing the child's true sex from her husband and the rest of the world. The child was given the gender-neutral name of Iphis. When Iphis was a teenager, Ligdus arranged for his "son" to be married to a local girl, Ianthe. Iphis fell in love with Ianthe and, as their wedding day approached, became increasingly anxious because, in Iphis's view (and indeed that of ancient Roman society), women could not marry women. Telethusa turned once again to Isis; she took her child to the goddess's temple and prayed fervently. As they left the temple, Iphis's body changed. Her stride became longer, her muscles larger, her hair shorter; in modern terms, Iphis's sex now matched his gender. On their wedding night, "Iphis the boy fulfilled the vows that [Iphis the girl] had vowed."[28]

The most troubling aspect is that there is no place in this myth for lesbian love; Iphis has to transition in order to stay in a romantic relationship with Ianthe. Iphis's reasoning is that "cows do not love cows, nor mares mares, but the ram desires the ewe. . . . In the entire animal world, there is no female smitten with desire for a female." It emerges from a long ancient tradition of drawing on examples from nature with which to naturalize heterosexuality and characterize gay relationships as abnormal, from Plato's *Laws* to the ancient Greek novel *Daphnis and Chloe,* and it anticipates similar homophobic arguments made in the modern world.[29] It is a pity that people making arguments from nature rarely turn to the example of the gorilla or the praying mantis.[30]

And yet, Iphis and Ianthe's tale ends happily. And the metamorphosis continues . . . from Ovid's story to Ali Smith's glorious novel *Girl Meets Boy.*[31] Smith embraces the Ovidian tale but also transforms it into a story that is free of the dodgier elements of the Latin poem.

In the modern adaptation—which is narrated in alternating chapters by Anthea Gunn (the Ianthe character) and her sister Midge (short for Imogen), who live together in the Scottish town of Inverness, where they work at a bottled water company—the focus is not on changing sex but the dissolving of gender boundaries. Anthea falls in love with an androgynous activist who spray-paints graffiti on the company walls to protest its selling something that should be free:

> My head, something happened to its insides. It was as if a storm at sea happened, but only for a moment, and only on the inside of my head. My ribcage, something definitely happened there. It was as if it unknotted itself from itself, like the hull of a ship hitting rock, giving way, and the ship that I was opened wide inside me and in came the ocean.
>
> He was the most beautiful boy I had ever seen in my life.
>
> But he looked really like a girl.
>
> She was the most beautiful boy I had ever seen in my life.

The girl is Robin Goodman, a name that fits the androgyny of her character and also nods to Shakespeare's Puck, the mischievous sprite also known as Robin Goodfellow, in *A Midsummer Night's Dream*. Like Puck, Robin is a wise agitator, and the novel, especially its fairy-tale ending, has a dreamlike quality to it. Robin's graffiti artist tag is Iphis 07, and she tells the ancient myth to Anthea, adding in her own comments as she does:

It's easy, when everything and everyone tells you that you are the wrong shape, to believe that you're the wrong shape. And also, don't forget, the story of Iphis was being made up by a man. Well, I say man, but Ovid's very fluid, as writers go, much more than most. He knows, more than most, that imagination doesn't have a gender. He's really good. He honours all sorts of love. He honours all sorts of story. But with this story, well, he can't help fixating on what it is that girls don't have under their togas, and it's him who can't imagine what girls would ever do without one.[32]

In this conversational reflection on Ovid, Smith acknowledges the problems with his account of Iphis and Ianthe and lightly and deftly moves on with her story, in which lesbian love does not require divine intervention. This is one of several self-aware moments in the novel, where the myth becomes not just the substance of the story but a process to ponder.[33]

In contrast to Ovid, Smith is not fixated with what is under anyone's toga (or kilt). When Midge, who has trouble dealing with the fact that her sister is gay ("My little sister is going to grow up into a dissatisfied older predatory totally dried-up abnormal woman like Judi Dench in that film *Notes on a Scandal*"[34]), asks Robin point-blank what is the "correct word for it, I mean, for you," Robin's response is a rebuke to Midge and to any reader who might be hung up on labels for sex and gender:

She looks at me for a long time. . . . Then, when she speaks,
it is as if the whole look of her speaks.

The proper word for me, Robin Goodman says, is me.[35]

In Smith's writing, and Robin and Anthea's loving, gender
dissolves; boy and girl lose their meaning:

She had the swagger of a girl. She blushed like a boy. She
had a girl's toughness. She had a boy's gentleness. She was
as meaty as a girl. She was as graceful as a boy. She was as
brave and handsome and rough as a girl. She was as pretty
and delicate and dainty as a boy. She turned boys' heads
like a girl. She turned girls' heads like a boy. She made love
like a boy. She made love like a girl. She was so boyish it
was girlish, so girlish it was boyish, she made me want to
rove the world writing our names on every tree.[36]

Perhaps the most brilliant aspect of *Girl Meets Boy* is that
it explicitly politicizes metamorphosis and restores people's
agency over their bodies and lives. In Ovid's tale, humans might
pray for themselves to transition, but it is the gods who con-
fer change, zapping transformation from on high. Robin and
Anthea spray-paint messages of feminist protest, emblazoning
them in public places around Inverness. Here are two of them:

ACROSS THE WORLD TWO MILLION GIRLS, KILLED BEFORE
BIRTH OR AT BIRTH BECAUSE THEY WEREN'T BOYS. THAT'S

ON RECORD. ADD TO THAT THE OFF-RECORD ESTIMATE OF
FIFTY-FIVE MILLION MORE GIRLS, KILLED BECAUSE THEY
WEREN'T BOYS. THAT'S SIXTY MILLION GIRLS. THIS MUST
CHANGE.

ALL ACROSS THE WORLD, WHERE WOMEN ARE DOING
EXACTLY THE SAME WORK AS MEN, THEY'RE BEING PAID
BETWEEN THIRTY TO FORTY PERCENT LESS. THAT'S NOT
FAIR. THIS MUST CHANGE.

They sign these with "Iphis and Ianthe the message girls"
or "Iphis and Ianthe the message boys."[37]

The novel weaves together and exposes the connections
among the joy of lesbian love, feminist protest, concern for
the environment (Midge eventually takes on the water company), and the fluidness of gender identity. It queers Ovid's
tale of Iphis and Ianthe, by which I mean that it takes a myth
that reinforces heterosexuality and with kindness and humor
rewrites it to affirm, instead, difference and diversity. It keeps
the radical elements of the ancient myth and changes the
rest. This metamorphosis is how Smith enables us to "escape
the prison-house of the story" and embrace a more liberating
narrative.

Unlike the groundswell of creative retellings of ancient
myths about homecoming, or the Trojan War, or Medusa,
or Lysistrata, or Venus, or Achilles and Patroclus, or Sappho,
creative adaptations of trans and gender nonbinary myths are
largely waiting to be written. *Girl Meets Boy* is a model for
what will hopefully become a trend and a tradition. There is

a thirst for this kind of transmythology. But the importance of *Girl Meets Boy* goes beyond that. It picks up some of the ideas that underpin this book. One of these is that desire is transformative. This can be destructive, as in the myths of the Earth-Ripper and his daughter, Apollo and Daphne, and Philomela, Procne and Tereus. But it can also be a force for the good, especially when, as with Robin and Anthea, strong personal desire is married to the desire for political change.

Change is within our control; unlike the ancients, we don't have to beg the gods for it. What are we going to do with that gift? *Girl Meets Boy* suggests some of the same answers as this book has done. By turning to the past, we can imagine our futures afresh. And that recognizing the subversive power of ancient myths—through reading the original stories closely and through enjoying their modern re-creations and using them to inspire and support political activism—can be both transformative and redemptive. As Anthea says:

> It was always the stories that needed the telling that gave us the rope we could cross any river with . . . they made us brave. They made us well. They changed us. It was in their nature to.[38]

CODA: ANTIGONE RISING

*Stories matter. Many stories matter. Stories
have been used to dispossess and to malign.
But stories can also be used to empower and
to humanize. Stories can break the dignity of a
people. But stories can also repair that dignity.*
—CHIMAMANDA NGOZI ADICHIE,
"The Danger of a Single Story," TED Talk

Somos muchos. We are many.
—SARA URIBE, *Antígona González*

THE COURAGEOUS *SPIRIT* OF ANTIGONE MAY LIVE ON IN
Malala Yousafzai, Olga Misik, and Greta Thunberg and
in the many young women who stand up to the misuses of
power, but the *story* of Antigone, as told by Sophocles in his
tragic drama, ends in catastrophe, pain, and ruin.

Antigone breaks the law and defies her uncle Creon, the
king of Thebes, when she buries her brother who was an enemy
of the state. When she will not back down, Creon orders that

she be buried alive in a tomb. (This is a particularly cowardly act: Antigone is left to starve to death, but because Creon has not ordered her immediate death, he hopes to avoid the religious stain that might arise from executing his niece.) Creon has a change of heart after a visit from the blind seer Teiresias who tells him that his actions have been immoral, but it is too late: when his guards go to release Antigone, they find that she has hanged herself inside the cave. Haemon, who is Creon's son and Antigone's fiancé, kills himself, and his death leads to the suicide of Queen Eurydice, his mother. Creon is left a broken man, but at what cost? As a script for successful activism, this story leaves quite a bit to be desired.

Antigone's lack of sisterhood is also a problem.[1] At the very beginning of the play, Antigone asks Ismene to join with her in burying their brother, but when Ismene voices objections to Antigone's plan, Antigone allows for no debate, disagreement, or compromise: "You will be my enemy," she says.[2] When Ismene attempts, later in the play, to share the blame for burying their brother and to be Antigone's ally, Antigone will have none of it. It is striking that in Sophocles's play, Antigone never says *we*. Toward the beginning of the play, she uses the formula *you and I* or *you and me*, and after that, her speech is all about *I* or *me*. Her language of exclusion reflects, and reveals, her politics.

Antigone's certainty and single-mindedness are part of her appeal. But certainty also breeds extremism, which, as Sophocles cautions, can be destructive. Today, Antigone's kind of intolerance and self-righteousness can be seen especially on social media, which tends to aggravate and inflame disagreements. Feminists are primed to call one another out, to punish transgressions, no matter how minor, to lack perspective, and to create a culture of silencing and shame. As Jessa Crispin puts it in her critique of modern feminism: "An environment where we strong-arm dissidence and varied opinion is an environment devoid of possibility and dynamism."[3] "Burn it down" is a catchphrase of keyboard warriors; it is easier to castigate and condemn than to persuade, inspire, and do the hard work needed to bring about positive change. There's a strand of nihilism in Sophocles's play *Antigone* that we would do well to reject.

One of the conclusions of this book is that ancient myths (stories) have subversive power precisely because they can be told—and read—in different ways. In the words of novelist Ben Okri, myths "always take wings and soar beyond the place where we can keep them fixed."[4] This can be due to their inherent ambiguities and their ability to reveal a different perspective if we read them with care (as we've seen in the way myths about sexual trauma, the environment, and gender transitioning in Ovid's *Metamorphoses* can be read in a new light). It is also due to the creative reimagining of myths by modern artists like Ali Smith and Beyoncé and by activists like Diana, the Hunter of Bus Drivers. These new adaptations change not only the plots of the ancient tales but also what they have to say about women, about race, and about human relations: in other words, in changing the myths (stories), artists subvert the myths (false ideas and beliefs) too.

Coda: Antigone Rising

The problem is that misogynist myths are more strongly culturally entrenched in our societies than myths that subvert them. The beliefs that women, especially foreign women, are to be controlled, conquered, and even killed, that some women deserve to be raped and will not be believed if they speak the truth about sexual violence are hardwired into our culture. The diet industry and the use of dress codes to control and punish girls and women and to enforce gender and racial norms are global social phenomena that cause immense damage and misery. The paradigms from antiquity that challenge these stories, beliefs, and practices are not as well established or widely implemented.

However, the creative adaptations of myth—the stories, videos, images, and novels that present radically different perspectives—are more than individual contestations: they amount to a formidable cultural trend. This was always the case: rewriting myth from different perspectives goes back to antiquity. Before Ali Smith, Spike Lee, Suzanne Collins, Mai Zetterling, and Beyoncé (and Inua Ellams, Madeleine Miller, Pat Barker, Ursula K. Le Guin, Natalie Haynes, and . . .) were Aeschylus, Sophocles, Euripides, Plato, and a whole host of later mythographers who delighted in recasting the stories told by Homer and in other (now lost) epic poems.[5] Subversive mythmaking is a process—one that involves the past and the present and all of the versions in between.

The Antigone myth is a good example of this. Euripides's play about Antigone, which no longer survives, almost certainly revised Sophocles's tragedy and allowed Antigone and Haemon to get married and have a baby son! Scholars' educated guesses, based on later summaries of the play, envisage wildly different endings for Antigone and her family. Perhaps Creon tracked them down, recognized them, and had them killed. Perhaps the hero Hercules intervened, and they all lived happily after, an ending that would have allowed Antigone to rebel against Creon's authoritarianism *and* to have a future.[6]

Even more shocking is the likelihood that in Euripides's version of the myth Haemon helped Antigone to bury her brother. She did not act alone. The possibility of Antigone taking collaborative action is also raised in an exquisite modern adaptation of the myth: a book (not exactly poem, play, novel, or newspaper article but containing elements of all these) called *Antígona González*, written by Sara Uribe and translated by John Pluecker.[7] It contains elements of, and meditates upon, previous Antigones in life, literature, and political theory, as it traces the journey of Antígona González, who searches for the body of her brother who has "disappeared" in Tamaulipas, Mexico, so that she can give him a proper burial. It gives us a sense of the long and rich tradition of using the Antigone myth to articulate abuses of power. Uribe's Antigone quotes a Colombian activist who took her name, even as she harks back to Sophocles:

> : No quería ser una Antígona
> pero me tocó.
> : I didn't want to be an Antigone
> but it happened to me.[8]

Coda: Antigone Rising

She fights a system, not a despot:

> *Supe que Tamaulipas era Tebas y Creonte este silen-*
> *cio amordazándolo todo.*
> *I realize Tamaulipas was Thebes / and Creon this*
> *silence stifling everything.*

The book draws on a long Latin American tradition that identifies Polynices with the marginalized, the separated, and the lost.[9] It evokes the mothers and fathers whom the US media calls migrants, although the mildness of that word erases their desperation, as they search for the children snatched from them by the country that they hoped would give them sanctuary but took their children instead.

A repeated refrain in *Antígona González* quotes Sophocles: "Will you join me in taking up the body?"[10] But whereas in Sophocles the character Antigone asks the question to her sister Ismene, in Sara Uribe's book, Antigone asks the question to us, the readers. Within this haunted question is a reminder that how the past influences the present and whether it is used to uphold or subvert brutality depends on us. Unlike in Sophocles's tragedy, Sara Uribe's Antigone insists on there being an "us" and an "us" with power.

Antigone is rising. Antigones (and Ismenes and Haemons) are rising.

Somos muchos. We are many.

AUTHOR'S NOTE

You don't need to know the Greek and Roman myths before reading this book. But if you want to read them, or re-read them, then Stephen Fry's *Mythos: The Greek Myths Retold* (Penguin, 2018) and *Heroes: Mortals and Monsters: Quests and Adventures* (Penguin, 2019) and John Spurling's *Arcadian Nights: The Greek Myths Reimagined* (Overlook Press, 2016) are excellent retellings, though, like all retellings, they take some delightful liberties. If you prefer to go back to the ancient versions, then Penguin and Oxford World's Classics have good, accessible translations. There is fascinating material in *Anthology of Classical Myth: Primary Sources in Translation*, translated and edited by Stephen Trzaskoma, R. Scott Smith, and Stephen Brunet (second edition, Hackett, 2004).

The names of the characters in Greek and Roman myth differ (Athena/Minerva), and some can be spelled in a dizzying number of ways. When I have gone backward and forward from discussing Greek to discussing Latin texts, I have stayed with one version of the character's name. Purists might not be happy, but I have wanted to minimize confusion.

ACKNOWLEDGMENTS

THIS BOOK HAS BEEN A PLEASURE TO RESEARCH AND WRITE, and I am immensely grateful to everyone who has helped.

My editor Katy O' Donnell has debated the ideas and arguments in the book with acumen and care. I could not have wanted for a better or more committed editor. I owe much to Brynn Warriner and her colleagues at Bold Type Books and to Kate Mueller for her excellent copyediting.

My agent George Lucas created the opportunity for me to write the book and came up with #MeTu. (I wish I had done so.) Johanna Hanink introduced me to George and has discussed the ideas in this book with me from the very beginning.

My colleagues and students at the University of California, Santa Barbara, have pressed me to think harder about why myth matters.

In the early stages of planning the book, I had fruitful conversations with Donna Zuckerberg. Donna is the founding editor of Eidolon, an online journal that publishes punchy, politically informed scholarship and journalism on ancient and modern interactions; its tagline is Classics Without Fragility. I am on the editorial board and owe much to Donna, her editorial team (Yung In Chae, Sarah Scullin, and Tori Lee), and the other members of the board (Johanna Hanink, Tara Mulder, and Dan-el Padilla Peralta).

Friends and colleagues have generously read and commented in detail on draft manuscripts of the book: Johanna Hanink, John Henderson, Simon Goldhill, Sara Lindheim, and Anna Uhlig. Emilio Capettini, Andrés Carrete, Mathura Umachandran, Caroline Vout, and Jessica Wright gave feedback on individual chapters, and Andrés also helped me with my research in Mexico City. Tony Boyle (who is also my partner) discussed the nuances of Ovid's Latin with me. They have all sharpened my thinking and saved me from errors; they are, of course, not responsible for any that remain. I have also had formative conversations with Bonnie Honig, Rose MacLean, and Max Rorty (who also went to see Beyoncé and Jay-Z in concert with me). The book is much better for their input.

Jennifer Louden, and the other participants in her writing group, helped to soften some of the academic stiffness of my writing and were unfailingly positive about the project.

My sister, Marina Castledine, has read my writing and sent me books to discuss. She, my brother Philip Lakka, and my friends Sara Lindheim, Margaret Prothero, Pascale Beale, Hillary McCollum, Sue Marsh, and Jennie Ransom have been immensely supportive.

Acknowledgments

Thanks, also, to Tony and Athena Boyle for being a family unlike those found in Greek myth, for many passionate discussions, and for their belief in the book. The kindness, energy, and clarity of vision of Athena and many of her generation give me hope for the future.

NOTES

PREFACE

1. Sophocles, *Antigone* 471–472; Greta Thunberg quoted in an interview with Jonathan Watts for the *Guardian* (Manchester, UK) newspaper, March 11, 2019.

2. See Helen Morales, *Classical Myth: A Very Short Introduction* (Oxford, UK: Oxford University Press, 2007).

3. See George Steiner, *Antigones: The Antigone Myth in Western Literature, Art and Thought* (Oxford, UK: Oxford University Press, 1984); Judith Butler, *Antigone's Claim* (New York: Columbia University Press, 2000); Bonnie Honig, *Antigone, Interrupted* (Cambridge, UK: Cambridge University Press, 2013); the chapters by Miriam Leonard, Simon Goldhill, and Katie Fleming in *Laughing with Medusa: Classical Myth and Feminist Thought*, ed. Vanda Zajko and Miriam Leonard (Oxford, UK: Oxford University Press, 2006); and Fanny Söderbäck, ed., *Feminist Readings of Antigone* (Albany: State University of New York Press, 2010).

4. Bryan Doerries is artistic director of Theater of War Productions, https://theaterofwar.com/projects/antigone-in-ferguson.

5. Ralph Ellison, "On Initiation Rites and Power: Ralph Ellison Speaks at West Point," in *Going to the Territory* (New York: Random

House, 1986), 39–63. See also Ellison's essay "Going to the Territory" in the same volume, 300: "It's as though a transparent overlay of archetypal myth is being placed over the life of an individual, and through him we see ourselves." I am indebted to Patrice D. Rankine's analysis: Rankine, *Ulysses in Black: Ralph Ellison, Classicism, and African American Literature* (Madison: Wisconsin University Press, 2006).

6. Ellison is especially interested in the construction of black identity. The quotation in fuller context in Rankine, *Ulysses in Black*, 127: "Mythology and folklore, like fiction in the novel form, allowed Ellison, a black writer in pre-Civil Rights, segregated America, to construct black identity from outside of a limited, contemporary framework. Although his approach garnered him much criticism, Ellison, through folklore and fiction, constructed human characters whose possibilities transcended the limitations that society placed upon them."

7. For more information on the Odyssey Project, see https://odyssey .projects.theaterdance.ucsb.edu/.

8. We are not certain of the date of the text. It might have been written after the date of Sophocles's *Antigone*, but if so, it still gives us an insight into the kinds of ideas about girls' behavior that were circulating. See Rebecca Flemming and Ann Ellis Hanson, "Hippocrates' 'Peri Partheniôn' (Diseases of Young Girls): Text and Translation," *Early Science and Medicine* 3, no. 3 (1998): 241–252.

9. Interview with Greta Thunberg, *CBS This Morning*, CBS News, September 10, 2019, www.cbsnews.com/news/greta-thunberg-climate -change-gift-of-aspergers/. See also Greta Thunberg's speech "Almost Everything Is Black and White," Declaration of Rebellion, Extinction Rebellion, Parliament Square, London, October 31, 2018, the text of which is printed in Greta Thunberg, *No One Is Too Small to Make a Difference* (New York: Penguin, 2019), 6–13.

10. See Esther Eidinow and Julia Kindt, eds., "Part III: Myths? Contexts and Representations," in *The Oxford Handbook of Ancient Greek Religion* (Oxford, UK: Oxford University Press, 2015); and Mary Beard, John North, and Simon Price, *Religions of Rome, Volume 1: A History*

Notes

(Cambridge, UK: Cambridge University Press, 1998). Not all ancient Greeks and Romans believed in the existence of gods and goddesses: see Tim Whitmarsh, *Battling the Gods: Atheism in the Ancient World* (New York: Alfred A. Knopf, 2015).

11. On the reception of Greek tragedy and other aspects of classical antiquity in different parts of the world, see Betine van Zyl Smit, *A Handbook to the Reception of Greek Drama* (Chichester, West Sussex, UK: Wiley-Blackwell, 2019); Zara Martirosova Torlone, Dana Lacourse Munteanu, and Dorota Dutsch, eds., *A Handbook to Classical Reception in Eastern and Central Europe* (Chichester, West Sussex, UK: Wiley-Blackwell, 2001); Almut-Barbara Renger, *Receptions of Greek and Roman Antiquity in East Asia* (Leiden, Netherlands: Brill, 2018); Barbara Goff and Michael Simpson, *Crossroads in the Black Aegean: Oedipus, Antigone, and Dramas of the African Diaspora* (Oxford, UK: Oxford University Press, 2008); and Kathryn Bosher, Fiona Macintosh, Justine McConnell, and Patrice Rankine, eds., *The Oxford Handbook of Greek Drama in the Americas* (Oxford, UK: Oxford University Press, 2015).

12. See Donna Zuckerberg, *Not All Dead White Men: Classics and Misogyny in the Digital Age* (Cambridge, MA: Harvard University Press, 2018); Alex Scobie, *Hitler's State Architecture: The Impact of Classical Antiquity* (Philadelphia: Penn State University Press, 1990); Thomas E. Jenkins, *Antiquity Now: The Classical World in the Contemporary American Imagination* (Cambridge, UK: Cambridge University Press, 2015); Simon Goldhill, *Love, Sex, & Tragedy: How the Ancient World Shapes Our Lives* (London: John Murray, 2004); Kostas Vlassopoulos, *Politics: Antiquity and Its Legacy* (London: I. B. Tauris, 2015); Page DuBois, *Slavery: Antiquity and Its Legacy* (London: I. B. Tauris, 2010); Jared Hickman, *Black Prometheus: Race and Radicalism in the Age of Atlantic Slavery* (Oxford, UK: Oxford University Press, 2017); and Edith Hall and Henry Stead, *A People's History of Classics: Class and Greco-Roman Antiquity in Britain 1689 to 1939* (London: Routledge, 2020).

13. Neville Morley, *Classics Why It Matters* (Cambridge, UK: Polity Press, 2018), 91.

Notes

14. On tracing "frail connections," see Emily Greenwood, *Afro-Greeks: Dialogues between Anglophone Caribbean Literature and Classics in the Twentieth Century* (Oxford, UK: Oxford University Press, 2010).

ONE

1. In antiquity, what territory Scythia referred to shifted; for more on this, see Adrienne Mayor, *The Amazons* (Princeton, NJ: Princeton University Press, 2014), 34–51.

2. *Antianeirai* ("equals of men") in Homer, *Iliad* 3.189 and 6.186.

3. Diodorus Siculus in Mayor, *The Amazons*, 253.

4. For the different versions of the myth and details of the ancient sources, see Marco Fantuzzi, *Achilles in Love: Intertextual Studies* (Oxford, UK: Oxford University Press, 2012), 279–286; and Simon Goldhill, "Preposterous Poetics and the Erotics of Death," *EuGeStA*, no. 5 (2015): 154–177. Robert Graves's poem "Penthesileia" describes how Achilles "for love of that fierce white corpse / Necrophily on her commits," in Michael Longley, ed., *Robert Graves: Selected Poems* (London: Faber and Faber, 2013).

5. Mary Beard, *Women & Power: A Manifesto* (New York: Liveright, 2017), 62.

6. Joseph Serna, Kate Mather, and Amanda Covarrubias, "Elliott Rodger, a Quiet, Troubled Loner Plotted Rampage for Months," *Los Angeles Times*, February 19, 2015. This kind of sympathetic language was common in the reporting. See also "the lovelorn loner" in Bonnie Robinson, Larry McShane, Rich Schapiro, and Nicole Hensley, "Santa Barbara Killer Elliot Rodger, Son of Hollywood Director, Vowed to 'Slaughter' Women Who Rejected Him," *Daily News* (New York), May 27, 2014.

7. Kate Manne, *Down Girl: The Logic of Misogyny* (Oxford, UK: Oxford University Press, 2018).

8. Manne, *Down Girl*, 19 (emphasis mine).

9. Ibid., 63 (original emphasis).

Notes

10. "Manless," Aeschylus, *Suppliant Women*, 287–289. Amazons rarely married. On the Amazon Atalanta being tricked into marriage, see Mayor, *The Amazons*, 1–13.

11. He suggests a different way of controlling women's sexual behavior in an epilogue to his manifesto: eradicating them, except for a few who would be kept for breeding purposes in laboratories.

12. Quoted in Nellie Bowles, "Jordan Peterson, Custodian of the Patriarchy," *New York Times*, May 18, 2018.

13. Euripides, *Herakles*, and Hyginus, *Fabulae*, 32. In some versions of the myth, Hercules kills his children but not his wife; see Pseudo-Apollodorus, *Bibliotheca* 2.4.12.

14. On the manifesto itself, see Sasha Weiss, "The Power of #YesAllWomen," *New Yorker*, May 26, 2014: "Rodger's fantasies are so patently strange and so extreme that they're easy to dismiss as simply crazy. But, reading his manifesto, you can make out, through the distortions of his raging mind, the outlines of mainstream American cultural values: Beauty and strength are rewarded. Women are prizes to be won, reflections of a man's social capital. Wealth, a large house, and fame are the highest attainments. The lonely and the poor are invisible. Rodger was crazier and more violent than most people, but his beliefs are on a continuum with misogynistic, class-based ideas that are held by many."

15. See Jesse Klein, "Teaching Her a Lesson: Media Misses Boys' Rage Relating to Girls in School Shootings," *Crime Media Culture* 1, no. 1 (2005): 90–97.

16. Strabo, *Geography* 11.5.3.

17. The suffragists thought that Amazons had really existed. Elizabeth Cady Stanton explained in 1891: "The period of women's supremacy lasted many centuries—undisputed, accepted as natural and proper wherever it existed, and was called the matriarchate, or mother-age" from "The Matriarchate, or Mother-Age" (1891), reprinted in Elizabeth Cady Stanton, *Feminist as Thinker: A Reader in Documents and Essays*, ed. Ellen DuBois and Richard Candida Smith (New York: New York

University Press, 2007), 268, quoted in Jill Lepore, *The Secret History of Wonder Woman* (New York: Alfred A. Knopf, 2014), 16.

18. The narrator introduces Wonder Woman in *All Star Comics* #8, written by William Moulton Marston: "She serves as a symbol of integrity and humanity, so that the world of men would know what it means to be an Amazon."

19. Translation from the French quoted in the Wikipedia entry for Marc Lépine, with a link to a transcript of the original letter.

20. "Education" for Boko Haram has connotations of Western, secular education.

21. Amanda Hess, "A *Thot* Is Not a *Slut*: The Popular Insult Is More about Race and Class Than Sex," Slate, October 16, 2014, https://slate .com/human-interest/2014/10/a-thot-is-not-a-slut-on-popular-slurs-race -class-and-sex.html.

22. Keith Hamm, "San Marcos High School Chat Room Participant Convicted," *Santa Barbara Independent*, October 3, 2018. See also Kacey Drescher, "Disturbing video threatening several Santa Barbara area students leaves parents shaken up," KEYT-TV, ABC, January 24, 2018, updated January 30, 2018.

23. Keith Hamm, "San Marcos Parents Spar with School District in Wake of Violent Video," *Santa Barbara Independent*, February 8, 2018.

24. Keith Hamm, "San Marcos Video Threat Lands in Juvenile Court," *Santa Barbara Independent*, May 10, 2018.

TWO

1. The play was first performed in 411 BCE.

2. For a general introduction to Aristophanes, see Paul Cartledge, *Aristophanes and His Theatre of the Absurd* (Bristol Classical Press, 1991).

3. *Flickorna* (The Girls), directed by Mai Zetterling, written by Mai Zetterling and David Hughes (Sweden: Sandrew Film & Teater, 1968).

Notes

4. Originally part of a trilogy of plays set at the RAF and USAF base at Greenham Common, Berkshire, UK: Tony Harrison imagined them being performed by the women of the peace camp. The trilogy was never performed. Part 1, *Lysistrata*, was first published in Harrison, "The Common Chorus," *Agni*, no. 27 (1988): 225–304. Then published as *The Common Chorus: A Version of Aristophanes' Lysistrata* (London: Faber and Faber, 1992).

5. First performed in July 1999 by Battersea Arts Centre, London, in association with the Steam Industry, and published in 2011 as *Lysistrata—The Sex Strike* by Germaine Greer, with additional dialogue by Phil Willmott (London: Samuel French).

6. The founders were Kathryn Blume and Sharron Bower. See Dorota Dutsch, "Democratic Appropriations and Political Activism," in K. Bosher, J. McConnell, F. Macintosh, and P. Rankine, ed., *The Oxford Handbook of Greek Drama in the Americas* (Oxford, UK: Oxford University Press, 2015), 575–594.

7. Maureen Shaw, "History Shows That Sex Strikes Are a Surprisingly Effective Strategy for Political Change," *Quartz*, April 14, 2017, https://qz.com/958346/history-shows-that-sex-strikes-are-a-surprisingly-effective-strategy-for-political-change/.

8. Alyssa Milano and Waleisah Wilson, "Alyssa Milano: Why the Time Is Now for a #SexStrike," CNN, May 13, 2019, www.cnn.com/2019/05/13/opinions/alyssa-milano-sex-strike-now/index.html.

9. Cowritten by Spike Lee and Kevin Willmott. See Helen Morales, "(Sex) Striking Out: Spike Lee's Chi-Raq," *Eidolon*, December 17, 2015.

10. Lines 149–154.

11. Jericho Parms, "Pray the Devil Back to Hell," Huffington Post, November 13, 2008, www.huffingtonpost.com/Jericho-parms/empray-the-devil-back-to-b-143734.html; and R. Weinrich, "Pray the Devil Back to Hell," Gossip Central, November 11, 2008, www.gossipcentral.com/gossip_central/2008/11pray-the-devil-back-to-hell.html. For other examples and longer discussion, see Helen Morales, "Aristophanes' *Lysistrata*,

The Liberian 'Sex Strike,' and the Politics of Reception," *Greece and Rome* 60, no. 2 (2013): 281–295.

12. Leymah Gbowee, "It's Time to End Africa's Mass Rape Tragedy," *Daily Beast*, April 5, 2010, updated July 14, 2017, www.thedailybeast.com /its-time-to-end-africas-mass-rape-tragedy.

13. Leymah Gbowee, *Mighty Be Our Powers: How Sisterhood, Prayer, and Sex Changed a Nation at War* (New York: Beast Books, 2011), 147. See further Joanna Kenty, "Lysistrata in Liberia. Reading Aristophanes's *Lysistrata* with Leymah Gbowee's memoir *Mighty Be Our Powers*," Eidolon, July 27, 2015.

14. The Accra Comprehensive Peace Agreement was signed on August 18, 2003.

15. E. Montes, "Colombia's 'Crossed Legs' Protest Is Redefining Women's Activism," *Guardian* (Manchester, UK), August 1, 2011.

16. "And so, like modern day Lysistratas, the women of Barbacoas banned sex from the town": Montes, "Colombia's 'Crossed Legs' Protest Is Redefining Women's Activism." See also Lola Adesioye, "Kenya Stages a Latter-day Lysistrata," *Guardian* (Manchester, UK), May 1, 2009; and Beatrice Dupuy, "Kenyan Women Hold Sex Strike to Get Their Husbands to Vote Their Candidate," *Newsweek*, October 23, 2017: "[Politician Raila] Odinga supported the modern-day Lysistrata strategy" (concerning a call for a sex strike in Kenya in 2017).

17. Donna Zuckerberg, "Sex Strikes Have Always Been about Patriarchal Power, Not Women's Rights," *Washington Post*, May 17, 2019.

18. Gbowee, *Mighty Be Our Powers*, 147.

19. This version of the Oedipus myth is found in Seneca's tragedy *Oedipus*. A character in the movie is also called Oedipus, but it is Chi-Raq who really plays the role of the tragic king. See further Casey Dué Hackney, "Get in Formation, This Is an Emergency: The Politics of Choral Song and Dance in Aristophanes' *Lysistrata* and Spike Lee's *Chi-Raq*," *Arion* 24 (2016): 111–144.

20. I have omitted a few lines that mention also gathering together people from the colonies.

21. Line 488.

22. Cinzia Arruzza, Tithi Bhattacharya, and Nancy Fraser, *Feminism for the 99%: A Manifesto* (New York: Verso, 2019), 7 (original emphasis).

THREE

1. E. M. E. Poskitt, *Practical Paediatric Nutrition* (Essex, UK: Butterworths, 1988), 282.

2. See Susan E. Hill, *Eating to Excess: The Meaning of Gluttony and the Fat Body in the Ancient World* (Santa Barbara, CA: Praeger, 2011); Christopher E. Forth, *Fat: A Cultural History of the Stuff of Life* (London: Reaktion Books, 2019). Christian Laes's article "Writing the History of Fatness and Thinness in Graeco-Roman Antiquity" is important, but he sometimes jumps to conclusions: *Medicina nei Secoli Arte e Scienza* 28, no. 2 (2016): 583–658. An important article on the subject is Mark Bradley, "Obesity, Corpulence and Emaciation in Roman Art," *Papers of the British School at Rome* 79 (2011): 1–41.

3. Hippocrates, *Prorrhetic* 2.24.

4. Hippocrates, *Regimen in Health* 4.

5. *Aphorisms* 2.44.

6. As I have argued elsewhere in relation to the controversial Virgil quotation on the 9/11 monument in New York City: David W. Dunlap, "A Memorial Inscription's Grim Origins," *New York Times*, April 2, 2014, www.nytimes.com/2014/04/03/nyregion/an-inscription-taken-out-of-poetic-context-and-placed-on-a-9-11-memorial.html?_r=0.

7. Roxane Gay, *Hunger: A Memoir of (My) Body* (New York: Harper Perennial, 2017), 137.

8. Chris Parr, "Sensitivity Training for Obesity Tweet Professor," The World University Rankings, August 7, 2013, www.timeshighereducation .co.uk/news/sensitivity-training-for-obesity-tweet-professor/2006382 .article. There are consequences for academics above and beyond being demoralized. A research study of fat female professors concluded that they feel compelled to overperform to counteract and compensate for

the perception that because they are fat they must be lazy: Christina Fisa-
nick, "'They Are Weighted with Authority': Fat Female Professors in Academic and Popular Cultures," *Feminist Teacher* 17, no. 3 (2007): 237–255.

9. Bradley, "Obesity, Corpulence and Emaciation in Roman Art."

10. *Chicago Tribune*, February 15, 1916. See further Ella Morton,
"100 Years Ago, American Women Competed in Intense Venus de Milo
Lookalike Contests," *Atlas Obscura*, January 15, 2016. A report in the "In-
tercollegiate Notes" of the student newspaper of Trinity College reports:
"The composite averages of the Swarthmore girls are said to be far nearer
the measurements of Venus de Milo than those of Wellesley, save that in
the ankle Wellesley is three-tenths of an inch nearer perfection. Swarthmore also claims an individual Venus, Miss Margaret Willets of Trenton,
N.J., who in every detail coincides so nearly with the measurements of
the famous statue as to make the difference negligible," *Trinity Tripod* 7,
no. 37 (March 3, 1916).

11. Her measurements were reported in Jane Dixon, "Being a Modern
Venus de Milo Has Its Disadvantages," *Sun* (New York), March 5, 1916,
https://chroniclingamerica.loc.gov/data/batches/nn_gleason_ver02/data
/sn83030272/00206534990/1916030501/0381.pdf.

12. See Margaret Justus, "Classical Antiquities at Wellesley College,"
Wellesley College Digital Scholarship and Archive, 2017, http://scalar
.usc.edu/works/classical-antiquities-at-wellesley-college/index.

13. The measurement cards and other information can be found in the
online exhibition *Building the Perfect Student Body* at the Peabody Museum of Archaeology and Ethnology at Harvard University, www.peabody
.harvard.edu/typicalamericans. See also Bruce L. Bennett, "Dudley Allen
Sargent: The Man and His Philosophy," *Journal of Physical Education,
Recreation & Dance* 55, no. 9 (1984): 61–64.

14. Cicero, *On 'Invention'* 2.1.1; Pliny, *Natural History* 35.36; and
Elizabeth Mansfield, *Too Beautiful to Picture: Zeuxis, Myth, and Mime-
sis* (Minneapolis: University of Minnesota Press, 2007).

15. The tale is told by the Roman grammarian Festus; see Adolphe
Reinach, *Textes Grecs et Latins: Relatifs à l'histoire de la peinture ancienne*

(Paris: Macon, 1921). See the reprint: Reinach, *Textes Grecs et Latins* (Chicago: Ares, 1981), p. 192, no. 211, under the entry "Pictor."

16. Why the Venus de Milo is an ideal beauty whereas women without arms are often objects of horror and pity is discussed by Lennard J. Davis, "Visualizing the Disabled Body: The Classical Nude and the Fragmented Torso," chap. 6 in *Enforcing Normalcy: Disability, Deafness, and the Body* (New York: Verso, 1995).

17. *Alison Lapper Pregnant* was displayed on the Fourth Plinth in London's Trafalgar Square from 2005 to 2007. Lapper herself tells how the Venus de Milo was an inspiration for her own life and work in her memoir *My Life in My Hands* (London: Simon and Schuster, 2005).

18. "Sorrows of the Fat" is quoted and discussed in Sabrina Strings, *Fearing the Black Body: The Racial Origins of Fat Phobia* (New York: New York University Press, 2019), 142–145.

19. Strings, *Fearing the Black Body*, 211. See also Christopher E. Forth, *Fat: A Cultural History of the Stuff of Life* (London: Reaktion Books, 2019), especially "Savage Desires: 'Primitive' Fat and 'Civilized' Slenderness," 207–235; and Sander L. Gilman, *Fat: A Cultural History of Obesity* (Cambridge, UK: Polity Press, 2008).

20. In ancient Greek thought, physical softness was one means of establishing cultural and geographical difference. Men who had soft bodies were believed also to have soft morals, and the environment played a role in determining both. In the Hippocratic text *Airs, Waters, Places*, we find the Scythians, a nomadic people of central Eurasia, described in terms that link their environment with their lack of physical rigor: "For neither bodily nor mental endurance is possible where the [seasonal] changes are not violent. For these causes their physiques are gross, fleshy, showing no joints, moist and flabby." See Hippocrates, *Volume 1: Ancient Medicine; Airs, Waters, Places*, trans. W. H. S. Jones (Cambridge, MA: Harvard University Press, 1923), 123–137. The softness and flabbiness of the Scythians are in contrast to the Greek ideal of strength and toughness. Even though physical differences are not used to inscribe racial differences, in our modern understanding of race, some of the

ways of thinking that underpin modern racism ("them and us" think-ing and the attribution of moral character to physical and geographical qualities) most certainly go back to antiquity, especially during and after the Greek-Persian Wars. See further Forth, *Fat*, especially 70–75. More generally on the constructions of race in antiquity and its impact on the modern world, see Denise Eileen McCoskey, *Race: Antiquity and Its Legacy* (London: I. B. Tauris, 2012).

21. See Linda Bacon, *Health at Every Size: The Surprising Truth about Your Weight* (Dallas, TX: BenBella Books, 2010); and Linda Bacon and Lucy Aphramor, *Body Respect: What Conventional Health Books Get Wrong, Leave Out, and Just Plain Fail to Understand about Weight* (Dallas, TX: BenBella Books, 2016). Fitness specialist and fat activist Ragen Chastain discusses how scientific studies frequently treat correlation as if it was causation; see Chastain, "Correlation Is Killing Us," Dances with Fat, July 20, 2011, https://danceswithfat.wordpress.com/2011/07/20/correlation-is-killing-us/.

22. Quoted in Laura Fraser, "My Sister's Cancer Might Have Been Diagnosed Sooner—if Doctors Could Have Seen Beyond Her Weight," STAT, August 15, 2017, www.statnews.com/2017/08/15/cancer-diagnosis-weight-doctors/.

23. Ellen Maud Bennett, obituary, Legacy.com, www.legacy.com/obituaries/timescolonist/obituary.aspx?n=ellen-maud-bennett&pid=189588876.

24. Hippocrates, *Epidemics* 1.

25. Carl J. Lavie, Richard V. Milani, and Hector O. Ventura, "Obesity and Cardiovascular Disease: Risk Factor, Paradox, and the Impact of Weight Loss," *Journal of the American College of Cardiology* 53, no. 1 (2001): 1925–1932.

26. www.intuitiveeating.org.

27. Aristotle, *Nicomachean Ethics* 1118b19–1118b21ff.

28. For a brilliant, searing account, see Gay, *Hunger*. For a wide-ranging discussion of why people become fat, see Anthony Warner, *The Truth about Fat* (London: Oneworld, 2019). Academic studies include Mark

Notes

F. Schwartz and Leigh Cohn, ed., *Sexual Abuse and Eating Disorders* (Bristol, PA: Brunner/Mazel, 1996); and Linda Smolak and Sarah K. Murnen, "A Meta-analytic Examination of the Relationship between Sexual Abuse and Eating Disorders," *International Journal of Eating Disorders* 31, no. 2 (2002): 136–150.

FOUR

1. See Kayla Lattimore, "When Black Hair Violates the Dress Code," nprEd, NPR, July 17, 2017; and Nadra Nittle, "It's Time to Stop Hair-Policing Children of Color," Racked, May 25, 2017, www.racked.com/2017/5/25/15685456/hair-policing-schools-braids-afros.

2. Julie Rasicot, "Why Do Teen Girls Dress the Way They Do?," *Bethesda Magazine*, December 1, 2008, www.bethesdamagazine.com/Bethesda-Magazine/November-December-2008/Why-Do-Teen-Girls-Dress-the-Way-They-Do/.

3. See also Sarah Bond, "What Not to Wear: A Short History of Regulating Female Dress from Ancient Sparta to the Burkini," *Forbes*, August 31, 2016.

4. See further Daniel Ogden, "Controlling Women's Dress: *gynaikonomoi*," in ed. Lloyd Llewellyn-Jones, *Women's Dress in the Ancient Greek World* (London: Duckworth, 2002).

5. Athenaeus, *Deipnosophistae* 521b; Phylarchus, *FGrH* 81 F54.

6. Anise K. Strong, *Prostitutes and Matrons in the Roman World* (Cambridge, UK: Cambridge University Press, 2016), 22.

7. Cicero, *Tusculan Disputations* 4.6.

8. Ville Vuolanto, "lex Oppia," in *Oxford Classical Dictionary* online, February 2019. This article has details of the ancient texts that discuss the Oppian Law, how scholars have interpreted it, and a further bibliography.

9. Vuolanto, "lex Oppia."

10. According to Livy, *History of Rome* 34.1. Ovid suggests a more brutal protest: the pregnant women stab themselves in order to induce abortions (*Fasti* 617–624). See also Plutarch, *Roman Questions* 6.

11. Of course, the repeal of the Oppian Law also benefited elite families who were in a position to accrue wealth; there was more than one reason why the law was repealed.

12. Deanna J. Glickman, "Fashioning Children: Gender Restrictive Dress Codes as an Entry Point for the Trans* School to Prison Pipeline," *Journal of Gender, Social Policy and the Law* 24, no. 2 (April 2016): 263–284. See also Artika R. Tyner, "The Emergence of the School-to-Prison Pipeline," American Bar Association, August 15, 2017, www.americanbar.org/groups/gpsolo/publications/gpsolo_ereport/2014/june_2014/the_emergence_of_the_school-to-prison_pipeline/; and NWLC, *Dress Coded: Black Girls, Bodies, and Bias in DC Schools* (report), National Women's Law Center, 2018, https://nwlc.org/resources/dresscoded/.

13. Kate Snyder, "Educators Weigh in on Ending School to Prison Pipeline for Girls of Color," National Education Association, August 29, 2017, educationvotes.nea.org. The article contains links to an interactive map that allows you to see the rates at which girls of color (black, Latina, and Native American) are suspended compared to white girls by state and district in 2015–2016.

14. Sufiya Ahmed, "Mayim Bialik, if You Think Modest Clothing Protects You from Sexual Harassment, You Need to Listen to These Muslim Women," *Independent* (London), October 17, 2017.

15. Cindy Davis, "Here We Go Again: North Dakota School Bans Girls from Wearing Pants So Teachers and Boys Won't Be Distracted," Pajiba, October 3, 2014.

16. The entire dress code can be found at www.eths.k12.il.us//cms/lib/IL01903927/Centricity/Domain/311/ETHS Student Dress Code Sec11 8-22-2017.pdf.

17. *The Bacchae*, by Euripides, directed by John Tiffany, Kings Theatre, Edinburgh, Scotland, 2007.

18. Euripides, *Bacchae* 228 in David Kovacs, ed. and trans., *Bacchae, Iphigenia at Aulis, Rhesus* (Cambridge, MA: Harvard University Press, 2003).

19. Euripides, *Bacchae* 310.

20. Ibid., 1134.

Notes

FIVE

1. Ovid, *Metamorphoses* 1.548–552.

2. On the names of the Galilean moons, see "Jupiter Moons," NASA Science: Solar System Exploration, https://solarsystem.nasa.gov/moons/jupiter-moons/in-depth/. Newly discovered moons of Jupiter are still named after figures from Greek and Roman myth, but after the god's children and grandchildren, rather than his victims: "The Results Are In! Jovian Moon-Naming Contest Winners Announced," Carnegie Science, August 23, 2019, https://carnegiescience.edu/news/results-are-jovian-moon-naming-contest-winners-announced.

3. Ovid, *Metamorphoses* 1.545–547.

4. See Bettany Hughes, *Helen of Troy: The Story Behind the Most Beautiful Woman in the World* (New York: Vintage Books, 2005); Ruby Blondell, *Helen of Troy: Beauty, Myth, Devastation* (New York: Oxford University Press, 2013); and Helen Morales, "Rape, Violence, Complicity: Colluthus's Abduction of Helen," *Arethusa* 49, no. 1 (Winter 2016): 61–92.

5. The Department of Justice National Crime Victimization Survey published in 2017 (of data gathered 2010–2016) reports that only 230 out of every 1,000 sexual assaults are reported to the police, out of which 46 lead to an arrest and 4.6 to conviction and incarceration, www.rainn.org/statistics/criminal-justice-system.

6. See Mike Vilensky, "Schools Out at Columbia, but a Debate over Trigger Warnings Continues," *Wall Street Journal*, July 1, 2015.

7. See Amy Richlin, "Reading Ovid's Rapes," in *Arguments with Silence: Writing the History of Roman Women* (Oxford, UK: Oxford University Press, 2014), 130–165.

8. The victims in Ovid are typically, but not always, female; see Richlin, "Reading Ovid's Rapes."

9. See Judith Lewis Herman, *Trauma and Recovery: The Aftermath of Violence—from Domestic Abuse to Political Terror* (New York: Basic Books, 1992), 99–103, 110, 111; and Kathleen Kendall-Tackett and Bridget Klest,

eds., *Trauma, Dissociation and Health: Causal Mechanisms and Multi-dimensional Pathways* (London: Routledge, 2009). Germaine Greer cites a Swedish study (published in the journal *Acta Obstretricia et Gynecologica Scandinavica*, May 2018) that "shows just how 'normal' it is for victims of sexual assault to experience a temporary paralysis that keeps them from fighting back or screaming. The researchers spoke to nearly 300 women who went to an emergency clinic in Stockholm within one month of a rape or attempted rape. Seventy per cent of the women said that they experienced significant 'tonic immobility,' or involuntary paralysis, during the attack": Greer, *On Rape* (London: Bloomsbury, 2018), 41–42.

10. Told in Ovid, *Metamorphoses* 6.412–674. On this episode, see Ingo Gildenhard and Andrew Zissos, "Barbarian Variations: Tereus, Procne and Philomela in Ovid (*Met.* 6.412–674) and Beyond," *Dictynna* 4 (2007), http//journals.openedition.org/dictynna/150.

11. Ovid, *Metamorphoses* 6.455–457. Even on the rare occasion when Ovid does spend longer describing the rapist's thoughts and motivations, the focus is on the man's obsession with the woman's appearance, words, voice, and virtue: Tarquinius's rape of Lucretia (Ovid, *Fasti* 2.761–812).

12. The details of which birds Procne and Philomela metamorphose into are not given in Ovid's description, but they are found in other versions of the myth. Ovid has Tereus turning into a hoopoë, but in earlier versions of the myth, he becomes a hawk: see P. M. C. Forbes-Irving, *Metamorphosis in Greek Myths* (Oxford, UK: Oxford University Press, 1990), 99–107.

13. As demonstrated in Ronan Farrow, *Catch and Kill: Lies, Spies, and a Conspiracy to Protect Predators* (New York: Little, Brown, 2019).

14. See Giulia Lamoni, "Philomela as Metaphor: Sexuality, Pornography, and Seduction in the Textile Works of Tracey Emin and Ghada Amer," in ed. Isabelle Loring Wallace and Jennie Hirsh, *Contemporary Art and Classical Myth* (London: Routledge, 2011), 175–198.

15. A point also made by Stephanie McCarter, "From Penelope to Pussyhats, The Ancient Origins of Feminist Craftivism," Literary Hub, June 7, 2017. The Pussyhat Project was criticized for excluding trans

women and women of color: see Julie Compton, "Pink 'Pussyhat' Creator Addresses Criticism over Name," NBC News online, February 7, 2017. Also relevant is the knitting website Ravelry, which has banned support for President Trump on its website because it amounts to support for white supremacy: Stephanie Convery, "'White Supremacy': Popular Knitting Website Ravelry Bans Support for Trump," *Guardian* (Manchester, UK), June 23, 2019.

16. Ovid, *Metamorphoses* 5.415–417.

17. Ibid., 425–427.

18. On Iambe, see Ann Suter, "The *Anasyrma*: Baubo, Medusa, and the Gendering of Obscenity," in ed. Dorota Dutsch and Ann Suter, *Ancient Obscenities: Their Nature and Use in the Ancient Greek and Roman Worlds* (Ann Arbor: University of Michigan Press, 2015), 21–43. On the *Homeric Hymn to Demeter*, see Helene P. Foley, ed., *The Homeric Hymn to Demeter: Translation, Commentary, and Interpretative Essays* (Princeton, NJ: Princeton University Press, 1994).

19. Photos published exclusively in the London *Daily Mail* newspaper, November 10, 2015, updated November 10, 2016, www.dailymail .co.uk/news/article-3303819/Inside-Donald-Trump-s-100m-penthouse -lots-marble-gold-rimmed-cups-son-s-toy-personalized-Mercedes-15-000 -book-risqu-statues.html.

20. The design is usually attributed to Angelo Donghia, but Chuck Chewning, the creative director of Donghia, Inc., for eight years, has suggested that an unnamed "casino designer" had more input into the final look: quoted in Jesse Kornbluth, "Before the Goldrush," BuzzFeed, January 16, 2017.

21. Two examples of these widely used metaphors: "Through the latter portion of the twentieth century, federal timber policy on the public lands was regularly criticized for despoiling virgin forest and prioritizing commercial timber harvesting at the expense of important forest habitat," from Bruce Huber, "The US Public Lands as Commons," in ed. Blake Hudson, Jonathan Rosenbloom, and Dan Cole, *Routledge Handbook of the Study of the Commons* (London: Routledge, 2019), 135–143;

"The people are there to protect Mother Earth from being raped and destroyed. . . . We must honor, respect and love our Mother for giving us life, land, each other, and ourselves," from Jessica Montoya, "Rising in Solidarity against the Exploitation of Mother Earth by the Dakota Access Pipeline," One Billion Rising Revolution, September 6, 2016, www .onebillionrising.org/37522/37522/.

22. As ecofeminists have observed: Tzeporah Berman, "The Rape of Mother Nature? Women in the Language of Environmental Discourse," in ed. Alwin Fill and Peter Mühlhäusler, *The Ecolinguistics Reader: Language, Ecology, and the Environment* (London and New York: Continuum, 2001), 258–269. A report in *Scientific American* concludes that, in the United States, there is a considerable gender gap in views on climate change and that many men view climate change activism to be a feminine activity: Aaron R. Brough and James E. B. Wilkie, "Men Resist Green Behavior as Unmanly," *Scientific American*, December 26, 2017, www .scientificamerican.com/article/men-resist-green-behavior-as-unmanly/.

23. Ovid, *Metamorphoses* 1.566–567. There is some ambiguity in these lines, but the Latin word *adnuit* typically means "to nod assent" rather than just "to nod."

24. As Jill Da Silva notes in "Ecocriticism and Myth: The Case of Erysichthon," *Interdisciplinary Studies in Literature and the Environment* 15, no. 2 (July 1, 2008): 103–116.

25. Juan C. Rocha, Garry Peterson, Örjan Bodin, and Simon Levin, "Cascading Regime Shifts within and across Scales," *Science* 362, no. 6421 (2018): 1379–1383.

26. In 2017 alone, according to Observatório do Clima (Climate Observatory), a nonprofit, climate change network, 46 percent of Brazil's greenhouse gas emissions were caused by deforestation of the Amazon: Dom Phillips, "Brazil Records Worst Annual Deforestation for a Decade," *Guardian* (Manchester, UK), November 23, 2018.

27. "Climate Change Is Making Wildfires More Extreme. Here's How," *PBS News Hour*, August 6, 2018; "Climate Change Is Creating Catastrophic Wildfires," World Economic Forum, weforum.org/agenda/2019

/05/the-vicious-climate-wildfire-cycle; and "Wildfires and Climate Change: What's the Connection?," Yale Climate Connections, www.yale climateconnections.org/2019/07/wildfires-and-climate-change-whats-the -connection/.

28. Iowa is 400 square miles; the area destroyed was 440 square miles. For more on the Thomas Fire, see https://en.wikipedia.org/wiki /Thomas_Fire.

SIX

1. See Stephanie Lynn Budin, *Artemis* (London: Routledge, 2016); and Tobias Fischer-Hansen and Birte Poulsen, eds., *From Artemis to Diana: The Goddess of Man and Beast. Acta Hyperborea* (Copenhagen, Denmark: Museum Tusculanum Press, 2009), 12. In Plato's *Cratylus*, the name Artemis is linked to the Greek word *artemēs*, which means "safe" or "unharmed."

2. See the *Homeric Hymn to Delian Apollo*.

3. Callimachus, *Hymn 3: To Artemis*.

4. Katniss Everdeen is part Diana, part Amazon. See Beverly J. Graf, "Arya, Katniss, and Merida: Empowering Girls through the Amazonian Archetype," in ed. Monica S. Cyrino and Meredith E. Safran, *Classical Myth on Screen* (New York: Macmillan, 2015), 73–82; and Helen Eastman, "Young Female Heroes from Sophocles to the Twenty-First Century," in ed. Justine McConnell and Edith Hall, *Ancient Greek Myth in World Fiction since 1989* (London: Bloomsbury, 2016), 211–224. More broadly on Greek myth as an inspiration for *The Hunger Games*, see David Levithan, "Q&A: Suzanne Collins Talks about 'The Hunger Games,' the Books and the Movies," *New York Times*, October 18, 2018.

5. Ovid, *Metamorphoses* 3.165–205.

6. Red Mesa de Muheres Juarez, www.mesademujeresjuarez.org/. See also Marti Quintana, "Mexican Women Take Action against a Growing Number of Femicides," EFE-EPA, August 18, 2019; and Michelle Lara Olmos, "Ni Una Más: Femicides in Mexico," Justice in

Mexico, April 4, 2018, https://justiceinmexico.org/femicidesinmexico/; and Patricia Olamendi, *Feminicidio en México* (Mexico City: Instituto Nacional de la Mujeres, 2016). Not all murders are investigated by the police: for further information, see observatoriofeminicidiomexico.org. Some scholars challenge the picture of Juárez as particularly violent toward women: Pedro H. Albuquerque and Prasad Vemala's 2008 study concludes that femicide rates in the city are no higher than those in cities like Nuevo Laredo. See "Femicide Rates in Mexican Cities along the US-Mexico Border: Do the Maquiladora Industries Play a Role?," SSRN Electronic Journal (November 9, 2015).

7. See Teresa Rodriguez and Diana Montané, *The Daughters of Juárez: A True Story of Serial Murder South of Border*, with Lisa Pulitzer (New York: Atrai Books, 2007). On the Toltecas bus drivers, see Alejandro Lugo, *Fragmented Lives, Assembled Parts: Culture, Capitalism, and Conquest at the U.S.-Mexico Border* (Austin: University of Texas, 2008), 233–248 (including extracts from local newspapers).

8. Rodriguez and Montaném, *The Daughters of Juárez*, 190–195.

9. Yuri Herrera, "Diana, Hunter of Bus Drivers," *This American Life*, WBEZ Chicago, 2013, www.thisamericanlife.org/Diana-hunter-of-bus-drivers/.

10. The architect was Antonio Rivas Mercado.

11. A similar story is told about another statue of a naked Diana, *Diana of the Tower* by Augustus Saint-Gaudens. It was placed above the Madison Square Garden Tower in New York City from 1894 to 1925, and it caused a scandal because the figure of Diana was naked. The statue is now in the Philadelphia Museum of Art. See Budin, *Artemis*, 163.

12. Alfonso Fernández de Córdova, "Cincuenta Años de Silencio; Diana Cazadora Vive!" (Fifty Years of Silence; Diana Hunter Lives!), Reportajes Metropolitanos, May 18, 2008, http://reportajesmetropolitanoes.com.mx/personajesyentrevist_mayo_08.htm.

13. Mario Larrez, "Del Caballito a Las Lomas" (From the Horse to the Hills), *Jueves de Excélsior*, no. 1222, December 6, 1945, 13–14, quoted in Claire A. Fox, "Lo clásico de México moderno: Exhibiting the Female

Body in Post-revolutionary Mexico," *Studies in Latin American Popular Culture* 20 (2001): 1–31.

14. The park was created in 1592. The fountains were commissioned under the government of Porfirio Díaz, whose aim was to put Mexico City on the same footing as other capital cities: statues with figures from classical mythology were part of that cultural grammar. During the colonial era, the park was for the enjoyment of the social elites only, but that began to change following Mexican Independence in 1821. By the end of the nineteenth century, it was popular with all social classes. The park was renovated in 2012, and street vendors were excluded from working there. See José Rojas Garciadueñas, "Mexico City's Fountains," *Artes de México*, no. 136 (1970): 22–78; and Carlos Villasana and Ruth Gómez, "Las Fuentes del Paseo Capitalino Más Antiguo" (The Sources of the Oldest Capital Walk), *El Universal* newspaper (Mexico City), March 4, 2017, www.eluniversal.com.mx/entrada-de-opinion/colaboracion/mochilazo -en-el-tiempo/nacion/sociedad/2017/03/4/las-fuentes-del. More generally see Andrew Laird and Nicola Miller, eds., *Antiquities and Classical Traditions in Latin America* (Hoboken, NJ: Wiley-Blackwell, 2018).

15. See Campbell Bonner, "The Danaid Myth," *Transactions and Proceedings of the American Philological Association* 31 (1900): 27–36.

16. Kelly Oliver, *Hunting Girls: Sexual Violence from* The Hunger Games *to Campus Rape* (New York: Columbia University Press, 2016), 121.

17. On women's anger, see Soraya Chemaly, *Rage Becomes Her: The Power of Women's Rage* (New York: Simon and Schuster, 2018); and Brittney Cooper, *Eloquent Rage: A Black Feminist Discovers Her Superpower* (New York: St. Martin's Press, 2018).

18. Andrea Dworkin, *Mercy: A Novel* (London: Secker and Warburg, 1990), 166.

19. As Jessa Crispin discusses: Crispin, *Why I Am Not a Feminist* (New York: Melville House, 2017), 39–44.

20. See the campaign group, We Stand with Nikki for more details, https://westandwithnikki.com/criminilization-of-survival.

Notes

SEVEN

1. This version of the myth is found in Hesiod's *Theogony* 166–206.

2. Botticelli's painting may have been inspired by *Homeric Hymn to Aphrodite*, a poem whose date remains uncertain but which was probably written a couple of centuries later than Hesiod's.

3. See further, Mary Beard, *How Do We Look: The Body, the Divine, and the Question of Civilization* (New York: Liveright, 2018); see especially "The Stain on the Thigh," 85–90.

4. See Christine Mitchell Havelock, *The Aphrodite of Cnidos and Her Successors: A Historical Review of the Female Nude in Art* (Ann Arbor: University of Michigan Press, 1995).

5. Meg Samuelson, *Remembering the Nation, Dismembering Women? Stories of the South African Transition* (Durban, South Africa: University of KwaZulu Natal Press, 2007), 86.

6. Sherronda J. Brown, "The NYT Review of 'Venus' Is a Reminder That Black Women and Our Suffering Are Often Invisible to Others," RaceBaitr, May 22, 2017, racebaitr.com. Brown's review is of a production of the play *Venus* by Suzan-Lori Parks (New York: Dramatists Play Services, 1998). *Venus* explores the relationships among Saartje Baartman, the audiences who came to look at her, and the doctor who made her tour around the continent and with whom she had a sexual relationship. On Parks's *Venus*, embodiment, and language, see Patrice D. Rankine, *Aristotle and Black Drama: A Theater of Civil Disobedience* (Waco, TX: Baylor University Press, 2013), 194–201.

7. The engraving was based on a painting by Thomas Stothard, which is now lost.

8. Isaac Teale, "The Voyage of the Sable Venus from Angola to the West Indies," in ed. Marcus Wood, *The Poetry of Slavery: An Anglo-American Anthology, 1764–1865* (Oxford, UK: Oxford University Press, 2003), 30. The poem was first printed in Bryan Edwards, *The History, Civil and Commercial, of the British Colonies in the West Indies* (1783) but was published anonymously prior to that (in Jamaica in 1765 and again in

1792). Teale was most likely an Anglican clergyman who had been employed by Bryan Edwards's uncle as a tutor to Edwards. Edwards grew up to be a member of the British Parliament and was pro-slavery. The poem makes reference to Sappho and Ovid, and in 1793 Edwards added an epigraph to the poem from Virgil's *Eclogues*. See Regulus Allen, "'The Sable Venus' and Desire for the Undesirable," *Studies in English Literature, 1500–1900* 51, no. 3 (Summer 2011), 667–691.

9. The final stanza was omitted from the 1792 publication.

10. If the response "it's fiction" does not suffice, then this article by Tim Whitmarsh makes some excellent points: "Black Achilles," Aeon, May 9, 2018, https://aeon.co/essays/when-homer-envisioned-achilles-did -he-see-a-black-man.

11. Under the art direction of Awol Erizku. On Jay-Z's appropriation of classical antiquity, see Dan-el Padilla Peralta, "From Damocles to Socrates," Eidolon, June 8, 2015, https://eidolon.pub/from-damocles-to -socrates-fbda6e685c26.

12. Beyoncé's pregnancy photographs were originally posted on her Instagram page. They have been reproduced in a number of places, including 1966 Magazine, February 7, 2017, https://1966mag.com/beyonce -pregnancy-instagram-photo-hits-10-million-likes/. Alongside the photographs was posted a poem by the London-based Somali poet, Warsan Shire, called "I have three hearts." The three hearts refer to Beyoncé and her pregnancy (she was pregnant with twins) but also to the transformation that is taking place as life grows inside the mother. The woman in the poem turns into Venus as she becomes a mother, and "black Venus" is celebrated alongside Osun, Nefertiti, and Yemoja; the poem helps us to interpret the photographs.

13. Audre Lorde's "An Open Letter to Mary Daly" is published in Audre Lorde, *Sister Outsider: Essays & Speeches* (New York: Ten Speed Press, 1984, 2007), 66–71.

14. See "Identity Europa," Southern Poverty Law Center, www .splcenter.org/fighting-hate/extremist-files/group/identity-evropa. On race, classical antiquity, and the academy, see further Rebecca Futo Kennedy,

"We Condone It by Our Silence: Confronting Classics' Complicity in White Supremacy," Eidolon, May 11, 2017, https://eidolon.pub/we-condone-it-by-our-silence-bea76fb59b21; Dan-el Padilla Peralta, "Classics beyond the Pale," Eidolon, February 20, 2017, https://eidolon.pub/classics-beyond-the-pale-534bdbb3601b; and Mathura Umachandran, "Fragile, Handle with Care: On White Classicists," Eidolon, June 5, 2017, https://eidolon.pub/fragile-handle-with-care-66848145cf29.

15. Donna Zuckerberg, *Not All Dead White Men: Classics and Misogyny in the Digital Age* (Cambridge, MA: Harvard University Press, 2018).

16. Within European traditions, the English and Germans have seen themselves as the true inheritors of ancient Greek civilization. On the exclusion of modern Greeks from this inheritance, see Johanna Hanink, *The Classical Debt: Greek Antiquity in an Era of Austerity* (Cambridge, MA: Belknap Press, 2017). On the problems of thinking about civilization, see further Mary Beard, *How Do We Look: The Body, the Divine, and the Question of Civilization* (New York: Liveright, 2018); Kwame Anthony Appiah, "There Is No Such Thing as Western Civilization," *Guardian* (Manchester, UK), November 9, 2016; and Silvia Federici, ed., *Enduring Western Civilization: The Construction of the Concept of Western Civilization and Its "Others"* (Westport, CT: Praeger, 1995).

17. On autochthony, see Vincent J. Rosivach, "Autochthony and the Athenians," *Classical Quarterly* 37, no. 2 (1987): 294–306; and James Roy, "Autochthony in Ancient Greece," in ed. Jeremy McInerney, *A Companion to Ethnicities in the Ancient World* (Chichester, West Sussex, UK: Wiley-Blackwell, 2014), 241–255.

18. Kara Walker, "Notes from a Negress Imprisoned in Austria," in ed. Johannes Schlebrügge, *Kara Walker: Safety Curtain* (Vienna, Austria: P & S Wien, 2000), 23–25.

19. "Catalog of paintings in the Louvre Museum," Wikipedia, lists the paintings as they are catalogued in the Louvre's Joconde database. See also Karen Grigsby Bates, "Not Enough Color in American Art

Museums," NPR, April 13, 2018, www.npr.org/sections/codeswitch/2018 /04/13/601982389/not-enough-color-in-american-art-museums; and the art activist work of the Guerrilla Girls, www.guerrillagirls.com/.

20. The Carters and Pharrell Williams (cowriters and coproducers), APESHIT, directed by Ricky Saiz, filmed May 2018, YouTube music video, 6 mins., posted June 16, 2018, www.youtube.com/watch?v =kbMqWXnpXcA.

21. Joséphine was a Creole woman who was born in Martinique. Beyoncé has sung about her own Creole identity in the songs *Creole* and *Formation*.

22. Jay-Z also explores this idea in his song "Picasso Baby" (2013).

23. "Brand New Ancients" is the title of a poem, written for performance or for reading aloud, by Kate Tempest, in Tempest, *Brand New Ancients* (London: Picador, 2013).

24. How you viewed the Sphinx depended on your cultural perspective. In the Egyptian mythological tradition, the Sphinx was benevolent. The name is said to have derived from the Egyptian word *shesep-ankh*, which means "living image of the king." As the Louvre commentary puts it, she was a "guardian and protector . . . defender of Egypt against hostile forces." In the Greek mythical tradition, in contrast, the Sphinx had a female head and was dangerous to humans. Sphinx is said to come from the Greek word *sphingein*, "to strangle"; she strangled men who failed to crack the riddles that she set.

25. The statue was previously identified as Cincinnatus, a Roman statesman who became legendary for his virtue and leadership. See Francis Haskell and Nicholas Penny, *Taste and the Antique: The Lure of Antique Sculpture 1500–1900* (New Haven, CT: Yale University Press, 1981), 182–184.

26. The more we know about African American visual art, the more resonant the video becomes. For example, the scene of hairstyling with the Afro hair pick echoes one of the photographs from Carrie Mae Weems's *Kitchen Table Series* (1990), and the dancing in front of the David painting is reminiscent of Faith Ringgold's story quilt *Dancing in the*

Louvre, on which see Dan Cameron, ed., *Dancing in the Louvre: Faith Ringgold's French Collection and Other Story Quilts* (Berkeley: University of California Press, 1998). See also Constance Grady, "The Meaning behind the Classical Paintings in Beyoncé and Jay-Z's 'Apeshit,'" Vox, June 19, 2018; Ariel Lebeau, "An Art History Expert Breaks Down Beyoncé and Jay-Z's 'APESHIT' Video," *Fader*, June 18, 2018; Sarah Cascone, "'I May Need to Lie Down': The Art World Goes Nuts over Beyoncé and Jay-Z's Louvre Takeover on Social Media," Artnet News, June 19, 2018; and Alejandra Salazar, "Beyoncé & Jay-Z's New Video Is a Major Lesson in Art History," Refinery29, June 17, 2018. More generally on Beyoncé and feminism, see Omise'eke Natasha Tinsley, *Beyoncé in Formation: Remixing Black Feminism* (Austin: University of Texas Press, 2018).

27. Rebecca Solnit, *Call Them by Their True Names: American Crises (and Essays)* (Chicago: Haymarket Books, 2018).

28. See the initiative Eos, which facilitates the collaborative study of Africana receptions of ancient Greece and Rome, www.eosafricana.org/.

29. See "Creative Time Presents Kara Walker," http://creativetime .org/projects/karawalker/; Matthew Israel, *The Big Picture: Contemporary Art in 10 Works by 10 Artists* (Munich: Prestal Verlag, 2017), 156–173; Rebecca Peabody, *Consuming Stories: Kara Walker and the Imagining of American Race* (Oakland: University of Calfornia Press, 2016); and Schlebrügge, ed., *Kara Walker.*

30. For Monae Smith, see UWB Zine Queenz, *Badass Womxn in the Pacific Northwest* (Creative Commons, n.d.), https://uw.pressbooks.pub /badasswomxninthepnw/; Dorothea Smartt, *Connecting Medium* (Leeds, UK: Peepal Tree, 2001); Kanika Batra, "British Black and Asian LGBTQ Writing," in ed. Deirdre Osborne, *The Cambridge Companion to British Black and Asian Literature, 1945–2010.* (Cambridge, UK: Cambridge University Press, 2016); and Laura Griggs, "Medusa? Medusa Black! Revisionist Mythology in the Poetry of Dorothea Smartt," in ed. Kadija Sesay, *Write Black, Write British: From Post-Colonial to Black British Literature* (Hertford, UK: Hansib, 2015), 180–181.

Notes

31. Robin Coste Hughes, *Voyage of the Sable Venus and Other Poems* (New York: Alfred A. Knopf, 2017). See also Dan Chiasson, "Rebirth of Venus: Robin Coste Lewis's Historical Art," *New Yorker*, October 19, 2015.

EIGHT

1. The story is told by the scholiast (ancient commentator) in Lucian, *Gallus* 19: see Hugo Rabe, ed., *Scholia in Lucianum* (Leipzig, Germany: Teubner, 1902), 92. The Greek play on the word *poiein* (meaning "to do or make") and Caenis's tricking Poseidon (Neptune) into doing whatever she wanted, making her (into) a man, reminds us of Odysseus's duping of the Cyclops (Poseidon's son), by telling him that "Noman" blinded him.

2. I am grateful to Hannah Clarke for sharing some of her survey responses before publication. She described to me how she conceived of the project: "I am very, very queer, both in a Sapphic sense and in the sense that my gender is complicated. I've got Sappho's name tattooed in the crook of my arm. My (unconventional, infused-with-artistic liberties) love of Classics in high school informed my understanding of myself . . . I knew that the language of Classics was something of a code for queer folk ('does he speak Latin?') and that people like me (a bit odd, overly enthusiastic, goth-of-center, and exquisitely gay) in fiction had a tendency to gravitate toward antiquity. . . . However, I found that the literature about queer reception of Classics was startlingly lacking. I thought I'd make my own." See further Hannah Clarke, "Queer Classics," Eidolon, July 23, 2019. For another testimony about the importance of Hermaphroditus and other nonbinary figures from classical antiquity, see Grace Gillies, "The Body in Question: Looking at Non-Binary Gender in the Greek and Roman World," Eidolon, November 9, 2017.

3. See Daniel Orrells, *Sex: Antiquity and Its Legacy* (London: I. B. Tauris, 2019). Turning to ancient Greece can be used to undermine gay rights, as in a US Supreme Court hearing in 2015 on the constitutionality

of same-sex marriage bans, when Justice Alito invoked ancient Greece as a society that did not allow gay marriage yet could not be said to be homophobic; see further Zachery Herz, "Law v. History: The Story of the Supreme Court's Misguided, Forty-Year Fixation on Ancient Gay History," Eidolon, June 25, 2015.

4. On the Oscar Wilde trial, see Alastair J. L. Blanshard, *Sex: Vice and Love from Antiquity to Modernity* (Chichester, West Sussex, UK: Wiley-Blackwell, 2010); see especially "Part II: Greek Love," 91–163.

5. See James Davidson, *The Greeks and Greek Love* (New Haven, CT: Phoenix Press, 2008).

6. On the relationship between Achilles and Patroclus in Homer's *Iliad*, see Shane Butler, "Homer's Deep," in ed. Shane Butler, *Deep Classics: Rethinking Classical Reception* (London: Bloomsbury, 2016), 21–48. On Achilles and Patroclus in the later literary tradition, see Marco Fantuzzi, *Achilles in Love* (Oxford, UK: Oxford University Press, 2012) with Butler's reservations. Madeline Miller's *The Song of Achilles* (New York: HarperCollins, 2012) is a moving modern novelization of their relationship.

7. See Daniel Orrells, *Sex: Antiquity and Its Legacy* (London: I. B. Tauris, 2019), especially 100–195; and Richard Hunter, *Plato's Symposium* (Oxford, UK: Oxford University Press, 2004).

8. See Margaret Reynolds, ed., *The Sappho Companion* (Basingstoke, UK: Palgrave, 2001); Jane McIntosh Snyder, *Lesbian Desire in the Lyrics of Sappho* (New York: Columbia University Press, 1997); Ellen Greene, *Re-reading Sappho: Reception and Transmission* (Berkeley: University of California Press, 1999); and Daniel Orrells, *Sex: Antiquity and Its Legacy* (London: I. B. Tauris, 2019), 126–151.

9. Vanda Zajko's article is an exception: "'Listening with' Ovid: Intersexuality, Queer Theory, and the Myth of Hermaphroditus and Salmacis," *Helios* 36, no. 2 (Fall 2009): 175–202.

10. See Luc Brisson, *Sexual Ambivalence: Androgyny and Hermaphroditism in Graeco-Roman Antiquity*, trans. Janet Lloyd (Berkeley: University of California Press, 2002), 7–40.

11. For Achilles and Deidamia, see Statius, *Achilleid,* and for Callisto and Jupiter, see Ovid, *Metamorphoses* 2.409–530, and *Fasti* 2.153–192.

12. Ovid, *Metamorphoses* 12.169–209.

13. *ita fama ferebat* (line 197) and *eadem hoc quoque fama ferebat* (line 200).

14. Akousilaus was a mythographer from the late sixth to the early fifth centuries BCE: *FGrH* 2 fr.22 [=P. Oxy. 13, 1611, fr. 1, col. 2, 38–96]. Καινῆι δὲ τῆι Ἐλάτου μίσγεται Ποσειδῶν. ἔπειτα—οὐ γὰρ ἦν αὐτῶι ἱερὸν παῖδας τεκέν οὔτ' ἐξ ἐκείνου οὔτ' ἐξ ἄλλου οὐδενός—ποιεῖ αὐτὸν Ποσειδέων ἄνδρα ἄτρωτον, ἰσχὺν ἔχοντα μεγίστην τῶν ἀνθρώπων τῶν τότε, καὶ ὅτε τις αὐτὸν κεντοίη σιδήρωι ἢ χαλκῶι, ἡλίσκετο μάλιστα χρημάτων.

15. The organization Human Rights Campaign tracks attacks on trans men and women, www.hrc.org/.

16. Ovid, *Metamorphoses* 12.470–476.

17. Sara Ahmed, "An Affinity of Hammers," *Transgender Studies Quarterly* 3, no. 1–2 (2016): 22–34.

18. Eddie Izzard, *Believe Me: A Memoir of Love, Death, and Jazz Chickens* (New York: Blue Rider Press, 2017).

19. See Anthony Corbeill, *Sexing the World: Grammatical Gender and Biological Sex in Ancient Rome* (Princeton, NJ: Princeton University Press, 2015), 112–135, referencing Michiel de Vaan, *Etymological Dictionary of Latin and the Other Italic Languages* (Leiden, Netherlands: Brill, 2008).

20. Macrobius, writing in the late fourth century CE: "In Cyprus, there is even a statue that represents Venus with a beard but wearing feminine clothing, equipped with a scepter and wearing masculine sexual organs and she is thought to be at once both male and female. Aristophanes calls her Aphroditus. [Another writer refers to her as] Venus the nurturer, [she is] both male and female . . . when offering her a sacrifice, men wear women's clothing and women men's clothing, because she is considered to be at once both male and female" (*Saturnalia* 3.8.2–3). Discussed in Brisson, *Sexual Ambivalence,* 54.

21. In Latin, apart from the original gods who had no gender, all gods and humans were given male or female pronouns. Grammatical sex did not map fully on biological sex.

22. Servius, *Aeneas* 7.498, discussed further by Anthony Corbeill, *Sexing the World: Grammatical Gender and Biological Sex in Ancient Rome* (Princeton, NJ: Princeton University Press, 2015), 119.

23. On the Teiresias myth see Nicole Loraux, *The Experiences of Tiresias: The Feminine and the Greek Man* (Princeton, NJ: Princeton University Press, 1995); see especially pages 211–226.

24. On Tiresias and the "orgasm gap," see Tara Mulder, "What Women (Don't) Want: Tiresias on Female Pleasure," Eidolon, March 19, 2018.

25. Jeffrey Eugenides, *Middlesex: A Novel* (New York: Picador, 2002); and Sarah Graham, "'See Synonyms at MONSTER': En-freaking Transgender in Jeffrey Eugenides's *Middlesex*," *Ariel* 40, no. 4 (2009): 1–18.

26. Eugenides, *Middlesex*, 430.

27. Ovid, *Metamorphoses* 4.378–379.

28. Ibid., 9.794. The tale starts at 9.666.

29. Ovid, *Metamorphoses* 9.731. On the trope, see further, Simon Goldhill, *Foucault's Virginity: Ancient Erotic Fiction and the History of Sexuality* (Cambridge, UK: Cambridge University Press, 1995), 46–111. For a more pessimistic reading of the Iphis and Ianthe story from a trans man's perspective, see Sasha Barish, "Iphis' Hair, Io's Reflection, and the Gender Dysphoria of the Metamorphoses," Eidolon, July 16, 2018. For Barish, it is other episodes of transformation that are most meaningful, for example the metamorphoses of Lycaon and of Io: "Ovid's descriptions of metamorphoses into animals resonate with the bizarre psychological state I've suffered for years, and with many other people's descriptions of [gender] dysphoria. Among works of ancient literature, it's these transformations that feel truest to my innermost feelings."

30. Gorillas are bisexual. The female praying mantis rips the head off the male after she has mated with him. For further examples, see this scathing extract from an article by Adam Rutherford, who criticizes the pseudoscience of trying to use animals' behavior to dictate what is

natural for humans: "The Human League: What Separates Us from Other Animals," *Guardian* (Manchester, UK), September 21, 2018, www .theguardian.com/books/2018/sep/21/human-instinct-why-we-are-unique: "You could compare us to killer whales. They live in a matriarchal social group, in some cases led by post-menopausal females. Or hyenas, the animal with the greatest jaw strength of any, which are also matriarchal, and engage in clitoral licking, to bond socially and to establish hierarchy. Or the insect order hymenoptera, which includes ants, bees and wasps, and are roughly the same evolutionary distance from us as lobsters. Their social hierarchy involves a single queen and males, whose role is two-fold: protecting the colony, and providing sperm on demand—they are literally sex slaves. Or the freshwater small invertebrates called bdelloid rotifers: millions of years ago they abandoned males altogether, and seem to be doing just fine." Iphis's arguments are wrong. For the attraction of female animals to female, and male to male, see Bruce Bagemihl, *Bio-logical Exuberance: Animal Homosexuality and Natural Diversity* (New York: St. Martin's Press, 1998).

31. Ali Smith, *Girl Meets Boy* (Edinburgh, UK: Canongate, 2007). The novel is part of the Canongate Myth Series, in which authors were invited to reimagine ancient myths for today. My analysis is indebted to that of Kaye Mitchell, in her chapter "Queer Metamorphoses: *Girl Meets Boy* and the Futures of Queer Fiction," in ed. Monica Germanà and Emily Horton, *Ali Smith* (London: Bloomsbury Academic, 2013), 61–74.

32. Smith, *Girl Meets Boy*, 97.

33. See especially Smith, *Girl Meets Boy*, 89–90, when Anthea asks: "Do myths spring fully formed from the imagination and the needs of a society, [. . .] as if they emerged from society's subconscious? Or are myths conscious creations by the various money-making forces? For in-stance, is advertising a new kind of myth-making? Do companies sell their water etc by telling us the right kind of persuasive myth? Is that why people who don't really need to buy something that's practically free still go out and buy bottles of it? Will they soon be thinking up a myth to sell

us air? And do people, for instance, want to be thin because of a prevailing myth that thinness is more beautiful?"

34. Smith, *Girl Meets Boy*, 56.

35. Ibid., 77.

36. Ibid., 83–84.

37. Ibid., 133–137.

38. Ibid., 160.

CODA

1. See Simon Goldhill, chapter 9, "Antigone and the Politics of Sisterhood: The Tragic Language of Sharing," in *Sophocles and the Language of Tragedy* (New York: Oxford University Press, 2012), 231–248.

2. Sophocles, *Antigone* 93.

3. Jessa Crispin, *Why I Am Not a Feminist: A Feminist Manifesto* (New York: Melville House, 2017), 102.

4. Ben Okri, *A Way of Being Free* (London: Head of Zeus, 2015), 44.

5. Inua Ellams, *The Half-God of Rainfall* (London: 4th Estate, 2019); Madeline Miller, *Circe* (New York: Little Brown, 2018); Pat Barker, *The Silence of the Girls* (New York: Doubleday, 2018); Ursula LeGuin, *Lavinia* (San Diego, CA: Harcourt, 2008); and Natalie Haynes, *A Thousand Ships* (London: Pan MacMillan, 2019). For ancient tragedians, mythographers, and other writers of myth, see Stephen M. Trzaskoma, R. Scott Smith, and Stephen Brunet, eds. and trans., *Anthology of Classical Myths: Primary Sources in Translation* (Indianapolis, IN: Hackett, 2016).

6. The fragments of Euripides's *Antigone* that have survived are in Christopher Collard and Martin Cropp, eds. and trans., *Euripides Fragments: Aegeus to Meleager* (Cambridge, MA: Harvard University Press, 2008).

7. Sara Uribe, *Antígona González*, trans. John Pluecker (Los Angeles: Les Figues Press, 2016). First published as *Antígona González* by Sur+ Editions, 2012. The 2016 edition is laid out with Uribe's text on the lefthand page and Pluecker's translation on the right. Actor and director

Notes

Sandra Muñoz commissioned Uribe to write the book in 2011; A-tar Company performed it April 29, 2012, in Tampico, Tamaulipas, Mexico.

8. Uribe, *Antígona González*, 175: "From the journal antigonagomez .blogspot.mx by the Colombian activist Antígona Gómez or Diana Gómez, daughter of Jaime Gómez who was disappeared and later found dead in April 2006, the autobiographical sentence: 'I didn't want to be an Antigone but it happened to me.'"

9. See, for example, Leopoldo Marechal's *Antígona Vélez* (1951), María Zambrano's *La tumba de Antígona* (1967), and Griselda Gambaro's *Antígona Furiosa* (1989). For other playwrights, discussion, and bibliography, see Uribe, *Antígona González*, 172–187. More generally, see Kathryn Bosher, Fiona Macintosh, Justine McConnell, and Patrice Rankine, eds., *The Oxford Handbook of Greek Drama in the Americas* (Oxford, UK: Oxford University Press, 2015); and Rosa Andújar and Konstantinos P. Nikoloutsos, eds., *Greeks and Romans on the Latin American Stage* (London: Bloomsbury Academic, 2020).

10. The translation used is by H. D. F. Kitto; see Uribe, *Antígona González*, 173.

INDEX

Index

Index

Index

Index

Index

Index

Index

Index

Patroclus, 104, 124, 126, 142

Peloponnesian War, 15, 20

Penelope, 72

Penthesilea, 2, 2 (fig.)

Pentheus, 62–64, 63 (fig.), 71

Pergamon, 52

Persephone, 73

   See also Proserpina

Peterson, Jordan, 7

Phaedra, 66

pharmaceutical companies,
   weight-loss drugs and, 42

Philomela, 69–73, 96–97, 143

Phoenicians, 108

Plato, 126, 138, 148

Pluecker, John, 149

Plutarch, 54–55, 57

Poland, women's strike in, 27

politics, inclusive, 26–27

Polynices, 150

Practical Paediatric Nutrition, 30

Praxiteles, 100

Pretty Woman (film), 60

Procne, 69–72, 96–97, 143

Proserpina, 73, 90

prostitutes, 55–56, 59–60, 125

protest

   APESHIT video as, 99, 111,
     115–117

   forms of, 93

   NFL player, 115–116

   taking up of space and, 111

public space, black people in, 111

pussy hats, 72–73

queer, 118, 123–124, 127–128

Queer Youth survey, 122–124,
   126–127, 135

Quinn, Marc, 40

racism/racial issues

   dress code policing, 49, 58

   exclusion of black culture from
     the Louvre, 110–111

   ideas of beauty, 41

   suspension rates, racial bias in,
     58

   underpinned by a cultural
     structure, 103–104

   use of classical mythology and,
     101–119

   Venus and, 103

Rankine, Patrice, xi

rape

   artwork depicting, 66

   Brett Kavanaugh and, 67

   by bus drivers, 86–87

   of Caenis by Neptune, 128, 130

   of Callisto by Jupiter, 127

   of Deidamia by Achilles, 127

   of environment/Earth, 77

   of Ganymede by Zeus, 126

   fear of for trans people, 131

   of Helen, 67

Index

Index

Index

Helen Morales holds the Argyropoulos Chair in Hellenic Studies at the University of California, Santa Barbara. She is the author of *Classical Mythology: A Very Short Introduction* and *Pilgrimage to Dollywood: A Country Music Road Trip Through Tennessee,* which inspired an honors history course about Dolly Parton at the University of Tennessee-Knoxville. Morales has been a guest on BBC Radio 4 *Woman's Hour,* and her work has been cited in the *New York Times* and the *New Yorker.* Morales taught previously at the University of Cambridge, where she was a Fellow of Newnham College, and has been a Fellow at the Center for Hellenic Studies in Washington, DC. She is on the editorial board of Eidolon, the popular online journal dedicated to antiquity and feminism. She lives with her family in Santa Barbara.